CONTENTS

STANDEN

West Sussex

THE NATIONAL TRUST

This book owes a great deal to the advice and example of the late John Brandon-Jones, for many years the house architect at Standen and the pioneer of Webb scholarship. I am also particularly grateful for the help of another Webb expert, Dr Sheila Kirk; and of the former Historic Buildings Representative for Kent and East Sussex, Peter Miall, and the former Administrator for Standen, Jane Grundy, who has patiently answered my enquiries amid more pressing calls on her time. John Bartlett has contributed the sections on the ceramics. Cathal Moore, Sallyann Morris and Robert Ludman wrote the garden chapter. The following have also assisted in various ways: Mary Bennett, Dr Neil Bingham and the staff of the British Architectural Library at the RIBA, Dr Terry and Mrs Mary Binns, Patricia Gill and the staff of the West Sussex County Record Office, Chichester, Cecily Greenhill, Archivist of the SPAB, Arthur Grogan, Barbara Morris, Mrs Elizabeth Motley, Mrs Linda Parry, Deputy Curator in the Textile Furnishings and Dress Department of the Victoria & Albert Museum, Miss C. L. Penny, Archivist at the University of Birmingham Library, Peyton Skipwith, and the staff of the City of Birmingham Central Reference Library (Local Studies Department).

The National Trust wishes to acknowledge the generous support of the Museums and Galleries Commission/Victoria & Albert Museum Purchase Grant Fund for acquisitions in 1982 and 1987 from the Arthur Grogan collection and in 1998 from the collection of Mrs Hazel Vickers.

Oliver Garnett

Photographs: British Architectural Library/RIBA: pp. 23, 26; Martin Charles: p. 9; *Country Life*: p. 13; E. Gray Dawber, *Old Cottages and Farmhouses in Kent and Sussex*, 1900: p. 11; Agnes and Rhoda Garrett, *Suggestions for House Decoration in Painting, Woodwork and Furniture*, 1876: p. 35; Museum of London: p. 16; National Portrait Gallery, London: p. 7; National Trust: p. 62, back cover; National Trust Photographic Library: pp. 31, 33; NTPL/Mike Caldwell: pp. 5, 17, 34, 51, 57, 64, 65, 69; NTPL/Roy Fox: front cover, pp. 36, 37 (left and right), 43, 68; NTPL/Jonathan M. Gibson: pp. 1, 27, 29, 30, 32, 52, 53, 60; NTPL/Angelo Hornak: p. 55; NTPL/Rupert Truman: pp. 4, 21, 22, 25, 49, 71, 72, 75, 76; NTPL/Derrick E. Witty: pp. 15, 18; R. C. Swift Photography: p. 41; Victoria & Albert Museum: p. 8; West Sussex County Record Office/Anthony J. Lambert: pp. 38, 40, 42, 45, 66, 74.

First published in Great Britain in 1993 by the National Trust
Revised 1996, 1999, 2001, 2002, 2003; reprinted 1997, 2002, 2004, 2006

ISBN 1-84359-039-5
ISBN 978-1-84359-039-2

Designed by James Shurmer

Phototypeset in Monotype Bembo Series 270
by Intraspan Limited, Smallfield, Surrey (SG1671)

Printed by Hawthornes
for National Trust (Enterprises) Ltd
Heelis, Kemble Drive, Swindon, Wilts SN2 2NA

INTRODUCTION

Standen is a house that reveals itself slowly. A narrow, high-banked lane winds down the hill past two substantial estate cottages. Through the trees you can just make out a complex roofscape of chimneystacks and clay tiles. The lane opens on to a broad green enclosed on three sides by an old weather-boarded barn, a tile-hung farmhouse and the modest service wing of the main house, with the complex east front towering above. Through a simple covered gateway is the entrance court, quiet and private. Only when you step out into the garden, to enjoy the glorious view across to Ashdown Forest, can you turn to take in the garden front and appreciate the special quality of Standen.

The house was built in 1892–4 for a prosperous London solicitor, James Beale, and his large family. He chose as his architect one of William Morris's closest friends and colleagues, Philip Webb. Webb built little because he built with such care. Standen is a testament to his love of fine craftsmanship and materials, and to his essential modesty. It enjoys the best of the views to the south, but, nestling into the hillside, does not dominate the prospect. Webb carefully preserved the existing old buildings on the site and made them the starting-point for his new house. It was built to last, of sandstone quarried from the garden, local bricks, hanging tiles, oak weather-boarding and render. All these materials were manipulated to create an eminently practical country house, but in a manner that is unmistakably Webb's.

Webb designed the interior of the house with the same care, paying equal attention to the needs of the family and their staff. He created light-filled rooms in which plain panelling was attractively combined with the colour and pattern of Morris wallpapers and fabrics. The Beales furnished the house with comfortable Victorian pieces and embroideries they had made with their own hands. Many of these are still in the house and have been augmented by sympathetic Morris & Co. furniture and Victorian and Edwardian art pottery.

Building a house is never an easy business, and Webb was not an architect to pander to a patron's fancy, but he got on famously with the Beales, who understood exactly what he was about and were delighted with their new house. Shortly after they moved in, they presented him with a silver snuff-box complete with a jokey inscription at their own expense: 'When clients talk irritating nonsense I take a pinch of snuff.' Standen remains the most down-to-earth of houses.

(Opposite) The south front

(Right) The fireplace in the Larkspur Dressing Room. All the chimney-pieces at Standen were designed by Webb specially for the house

5

CHAPTER ONE

THE ARCHITECT

*He did, or tried to do, for building what Browning
attempted for poetry: to revitalize it by returning to
contact with reality.*

W. R. Lethaby

Early in 1856 the 25-year-old Philip Webb met the
22-year-old William Morris for the first time: 'we
understood one another at once', Morris said later.
From that understanding grew the Morris company
which was to transform the standard of interior
design in Britain and to play a central role in the Arts
and Crafts movement. But while Morris's achievements have been exhaustively analysed, Webb is an
almost forgotten figure. His career deserves to be
much better known. Standen, one of his last and
least altered country houses, cannot be fully appreciated without knowing something of this quiet
man. And as a pioneer in the campaign to save
Britain's ancient buildings, Webb was among the
spiritual fathers of the National Trust.

Webb was born in Oxford in 1831 and christened
Philippe after France's liberal new king, Louis-
Philippe. His father was a country doctor who
enjoyed spending an evening snipping out intricate
paper animals with scissors. Webb gained from his
father a love of the natural world. Many years later
he said, 'To draw animals you must sympathise
with them; you must know what it feels like to be an
animal.' He was to approach all his later architectural work in the same spirit, always trying to adopt
the point of view of the people who would have to
use it.

The Oxford of the 1830s in which Webb grew up
was still largely a city of ancient buildings untainted
by the modern world; the railway only arrived
when Webb was thirteen. Oxford taught Webb to
revere good architecture, whether grand or humble, and to appreciate the beauty of traditional
materials and craftsmanship. He said of Oxford,

'That place is mine and I am of it.' After a three-year
apprenticeship from 1848 with John Billing in
Reading, he briefly entered another architect's
office in Wolverhampton. The town's grisly Victorian slums, 'those rows of infernal dog holes',
came as a shock after Oxford. The memory stayed
with him for the rest of his life and helped to shape
his strong views on the social consequences of bad
housing.

Webb returned with relief to Oxford where he
became chief assistant to George Edmund Street,
who had been appointed the diocesan architect in
1852. Street was one of the most able of the High
Victorian architects who made Gothic the approved
style not only for the innumerable new churches
that were springing up all over the country, but also
for country houses, public buildings and factories.
He is today probably best remembered for the Law
Courts in the Strand, London. Street's Oxford
practice entailed much restoration of old churches,
and Webb was often sent out to draw detailed
surveys of them. The work developed his skill as a
draughtsman and increased still further his understanding and love of traditional stone- and wood-
carving techniques. Like most successful Victorian
architects, Street ran a busy office, but he was
unusual in designing almost every feature of his
buildings himself, leaving only the more routine
work to Webb and his other assistants. Long hours
at the drawing-board were, however, lightened by
occasional high jinks. One of Street's pupils, a
baronet's son, spent much of his time balancing on
his head on a coal scuttle.

William Morris, just down from Exeter College,
Oxford, joined the Street office in 1856, determined
to become an architect. Webb soon made friends
with the young Morris, 'a slim boy like a wonderful
bird just out of his shell'; the friendship was to be
lifelong. They found that they shared a fascination

Philip Webb, the architect of Standen; watercolour by Charles Fairfax Murray, 1873 (National Portrait Gallery)

Oxford as it would have looked in Webb's youth; watercolour of the High Street by A. C. Pugin, 1814 (Victoria & Albert Museum)

with medieval architecture and the ideas of John Ruskin. The previous year Webb had bought a copy of *The Stones of Venice*, in which Ruskin celebrated the medieval ideal of unselfconscious craftsmanship, in contrast to the bastardised standards of modern industrial design. They went for dips in the Cherwell at dawn and sketching trips into the Oxfordshire countryside. Webb taught Morris the practical aspects of building construction, and together they developed the ideas about art and society that Morris was to expound in his writings and lectures.

Together they followed Street when he moved his office to London in August 1856. Morris soon abandoned architecture and set up home in Red

Lion Square with his old university friend Edward Burne-Jones. Unhappy with the conservative furniture then being produced commercially, he attempted to design new pieces for their lodgings in the medieval style he loved so much. However, the crude, uncomfortable results convinced him that his talents did not lie in furniture-making. So he turned to Webb, who built him a large cabinet with corner-shafts and crenellated top inspired by medieval architecture (now in the Victoria & Albert Museum). The flat front and side panels were reserved for scenes from Chaucer's *Prioress's Tale* painted in a vaguely medieval style by Burne-Jones. From these tentative beginnings were to grow all Webb's furniture designs for Morris & Co.

In 1858 Morris married Jane Burden and decided to move out of London to Bexleyheath in Kent. On a rowing trip together down the Seine sketching French cathedrals, Morris asked Webb to 'build me a house very medieval in spirit'. The Red House has traditionally been seen as a building of international importance, one of the seeds of the Arts and Crafts movement. But when first built, it had almost no influence, and indeed many of its seemingly novel features can be traced to other buildings of the period. The hipped gables, dormer windows and tall chimneystacks, the red brick and large areas of tiled roof were all being used by Street and another of the High Victorian 'Goths', William Butterfield, in their village schools and parsonages of the 1850s. Morris considered the Red House to be 'in the style of the thirteenth century', and it does have a number of Early English pointed windows, but Webb was always more interested in the functional potential of Gothic architecture, as championed by A. W. N. Pugin, than in its stylistic trimmings. His aim, as in all his later buildings, was to create a practical home of a sensible size, well-built from traditional materials. He therefore paid particular attention to the plan, which placed the kitchen on the same floor and conveniently close to the dining-room – an unusual arrangement at this period. The kitchen windows also allowed the servants to look out over the garden, not something most Victorian clients would have allowed.

Although Webb placed the windows to suit the plan rather than external symmetry, the main rooms face north and so are somewhat gloomy. But this hardly worried Morris, who wanted the Red

Red House, Bexleyheath, Kent

House to have the sombre glow of a medieval palace. The rich decoration and furnishings certainly gave it that atmosphere. Stained glass, with little birds drawn by Webb, decorated some of the windows. The ceiling of the staircase hall was pricked out with an abstract design of startling modernity, stencilled in bright blue and green distemper. Murals or tapestries covered the walls, Persian carpets the floor. Webb designed more tables and dressers in a solid, simple Gothic style, and also had a hand in creating the candlesticks and fire-irons, light-fittings and tableware that Morris wanted made anew in a medieval spirit. D. G. Rossetti described Red House as 'more a poem than a house. . . but an admirable place to live in too'; the qualification would have pleased Webb's practical nature.

Out of the task of furnishing Red House grew Morris, Marshall, Faulkner & Co., which was founded in April 1861 as 'Fine Art Workmen in Painting, Carving, Furniture and the Metals'. Morris provided the inspiration and most of the cash; Burne-Jones, Rossetti and Ford Madox Brown the figure designs. Webb, who was another of the founding members, made sure that the firm's products did not fall apart. He designed most of the early Morris & Co. furniture, which was usually of plain oak, often stained black or green, or decorated with gesso, oil paint or lacquer. He was also largely responsible for the setting-out and production of the firm's stained-glass work.

Somewhat naïvely, Morris & Co.'s first prospectus promised to offer its wares 'at the smallest possible expense'. However, such labour-intensive craftsmanship did not come cheap, and as Morris was not prepared to compromise standards, he found himself 'ministering to the swinish luxury of the rich', as he put it. In the early years the firm depended very largely for its survival on stained-glass commissions from G. F. Bodley, but Webb ensured that clients for his buildings went to Morris & Co. for their furnishings. After the firm was restructured in 1875, Morris took over more day-to-day control, but Webb still remained closely involved as designer, consultant and patron.

Although Red House was unique, built to satisfy the very individual needs of William Morris, it was

to have a decisive influence on the whole of Webb's subsequent career as an independent architect. It is difficult to imagine now, when Red House is surrounded by suburban semis, but it was built as a country house, and almost all of Webb's most important commissions were to be for country houses. He designed very few public or commercial buildings, and only one church. Webb was temperamentally incapable of the compromise and flattery necessary to win over a building committee. A private man, he very rarely allowed his buildings to be published in the architectural press and hated the publicity involved in such commissions, preferring to work quietly for a single sympathetic client. Most were, like Morris, artists – Val Prinsep, Spencer Stanhope, G. F. Watts and George Price Boyce – or were drawn from a small circle of art-loving families, who came back to him again and again; the Wyndhams, Howards and Bells were his most loyal patrons. Webb wrote later, '. . . for some time I have decided not to undertake to build for anyone who is not conversant with my work and able to judge of what would be the finished effect of that which I should agree to carry out.'

Compared to Street and the other great High Victorian architects, Webb built little. He employed only two trusted assistants in his spartan office in Raymond Buildings, Gray's Inn, which had neither typewriter nor telephone. He preferred to design every element of his houses himself, down to the smallest decorative detail. Therein lies the paradoxical flaw at the heart of the Arts and Crafts movement. For such close supervision might improve standards, but it also restricted the artistic freedom of the craftsman – the very freedom that he, and Ruskin before him, had recognised as essential to the achievements of the medieval craftsman.

Webb very quickly abandoned the more obvious Gothic features of Red House. Reacting against the

(Opposite) One of the ancient weather-boarded cottages facing the church at Penshurst in Kent, with, to the left, part of George Devey's tile-hung extension of 1848–50; photograph by W. Galsworthy Davie, a pupil of William Butterfield, from Old Cottages and Farmhouses in Kent and Sussex *(1900)*

'Battle of the Styles' between Classical and Gothic that had dominated early Victorian architecture, he sought to create houses that would be true to his own, modern age, but which would also draw on the best elements of Britain's native building tradition.

The story of the Vernacular Revival, in which Webb was to play a central part, really begins ten miles north-east of Standen at Penshurst in Kent. Here from 1848 to 1850 George Devey was commissioned by Lord de l'Isle to extend a group of ancient tile-hung and weather-boarded cottages beside the village church. He did so with such skill that today, 150 years later, it is hard to distinguish old from new, despite the date '1850' impressed into the roughcast walls. The supremely picturesque silhouette of the cottage roofs and chimneys, with the tower of St John the Baptist church behind, betrays Devey's early training with the water-colourists John Sell Cotman and J. D. Harding. In his youth Webb had also studied Harding's drawing manual, which drew his attention to the texture of weathered stone and wood.

Four miles south of Penshurst, Richard Norman Shaw built a pair of country houses in the later 1860s, Leyswood and Glen Andred, that ensured the popularity of the 'Old English' style, as it came to be known. Shaw had succeeded Webb as Street's chief assistant in 1858, and was to be the most successful country house architect in late Victorian Britain. At Leyswood (now mostly demolished) he combined the elements of the traditional Wealden house – red brick, tile-hanging, half-timbered gable ends, leaded light windows – with extraordinary brio to create a complex roofscape of varying levels and angles, anchored by tall, intricately modelled chimneystacks. The result had the 'quaint' aura of one of Joseph Nash's *Mansions of England in the Olden Time*, but with all the conveniences of a modern home. Shaw's seductive perspectives of Leyswood, which subtly exaggerated both the size and drama of the house, were exhibited at the Royal Academy and published to widespread acclaim.

Webb respected Shaw, but was never close. He lacked Shaw's suavity, both as a person and an architect. He was also not interested in achieving such a huge practice or in the courting of bossy plutocrats that it entailed. Webb certainly influenced Shaw, but also appears to have learnt from his buildings. He manipulated traditional forms and materials with the same freedom, but with less concern for picturesque effect. The layout of Standen around three sides of a courtyard, reached through a gateway in the service buildings, also seems to echo Leyswood. But, for the most part, Webb went his own way.

Clouds, near East Knoyle in Wiltshire, was probably the finest of Webb's later houses, but has been badly mutilated. It was built between 1881 and 1886 for the Hon. Percy and Madeline Wyndham, and for a particular way of life. The Wyndhams were members of 'the Souls', a group of intellectually inclined aristocrats that included A. J. Balfour and George Curzon. Their life centred on country house parties in which political and emotional alliances were made and unmade amid high-minded talk. Webb planned Clouds around a high-ceilinged, top-lit hall, which was intended to be the focus for these parties. The other principal rooms were equally spacious and flooded with light. In contrast to Red House, the decoration was sparing, being restricted to simple plasterwork, based very loosely on Classical Greek and Byzantine models, in the drawing-room and pale oak panelling in the dining-room, all designed by Webb. Morris wallpapers were reserved for the private rooms and furniture kept to a minimum. White paint predominated. Percy Wyndham called Clouds 'the house of the age', and few buildings better symbolise the enlightened late Victorian world of 'the Souls'.

In designing the exterior Webb spent many weeks studying local buildings and incorporated a number of their features, for example the flat relieving arches above the stone lintels of the top windows. The house is also built from green sandstone dug from local quarries. However, unlike Devey at Penshurst or to a lesser extent Shaw's Leyswood, Webb never tried to deceive. Clouds is an unashamedly modern house, and indeed it could only have been designed by Webb. The round-headed sash-windows and the grouped and weather-boarded gable ends are particularly unmistakable Webbisms. Although on a much larger

The Drawing Room at Clouds in Wiltshire in 1904

scale than Red House, Clouds was still a modest building. As he said once, 'I never begin to be satisfied until my work looks commonplace.'

When not building new homes, Webb was much involved in saving the best of the old. In 1877 he became a founder member of 'Anti-Scrape', the Society for the Protection of Ancient Buildings, which was set up to challenge the crude 'restoration' methods of many Victorian architects. While Morris agitated, Webb provided practical solutions, devising new techniques for saving threatened buildings without destroying their surface texture. Webb's work for the SPAB led to the passing of the Ancient Monuments Protection Act in 1882 and, indirectly, to the foundation of the National Trust thirteen years later. Over supper at Gatti's restaurant after SPAB meetings, Webb also inspired a whole

generation of Arts and Crafts architects with his ideas, including W. R. Lethaby, the first director of the Central School of Arts and Crafts, and many of the members of the pioneering LCC architects' department.

Webb had, on occasion, to restore his own work. In January 1889, only two years after Clouds had been completed, the greater part of it was destroyed by fire. While Webb set about rebuilding, the Wyndham family retreated to the undamaged servants' wing. Mrs Wyndham wrote to a friend, 'It is a good thing that our architect was a Socialist, because we find ourselves just as comfortable in the servants' quarters as we were in our own.' As the rebuilding work neared completion, Webb received a visitor at Raymond Buildings. On 20 March 1891 he noted in his office account book, 'Mr Beale first called here to ask me to advise him, and design a house etc. for Hollybush Farm.'

CHAPTER TWO
THE CLIENT

He was first and foremost a 'railway man'.

The Times

James Samuel Beale came from one of the great Birmingham families. There had been Beales in Birmingham since at least 1700. By the mid-nineteenth century they and a small number of other Unitarian families – the Kenricks, Phipsons, Huttons and, most famously, the Chamberlains – dominated the upper rungs of Birmingham society and the business life of the town. With the explosive growth of Birmingham as the manufacturing centre of nineteenth-century Britain, these families prospered. They intermarried and moved into the grander sort of houses in the leafy Birmingham suburb of Edgbaston, where James Beale was born in 1840. The comfortable Edgbaston world in which Beale grew up is powerfully evoked in the 'Alvaston' novels of Francis Brett Young. The Liberal Unitarian Lacey family in *Dr Bradley Remembers* (1938) might easily have been the Beales:

Unlike most of their wealthy neighbours, these people had not been satisfied with the mere making of money . . . They bought pictures, built music-rooms, amassed libraries, of which they were proud, and maintained an eager and vivid interest in the latest development of the Arts and Sciences, which they subsidized liberally but without ostentation; they were, in short, the fine flower of the new industrial aristocracy.

There were few aspects of Birmingham's civic life in which the Beale family did not participate. James's uncle, Samuel, was mayor of the town in 1841. His elder brother, William Phipson, a QC and amateur mineralogist, was much involved in local Liberal politics. His younger brother, Charles Gabriel, was perhaps the most influential: lord mayor three times, architect of the Elan Valley waterworks scheme, mastermind of the tramway system, chairman of the triennial Music Festival,

supporter of the Shakespeare Reading Society and the non-denominational Edgbaston High School for Girls, and first vice-chancellor of Birmingham University, which he helped to found in 1900.

The main family business was the solicitors Beale & Co., which was headed in the mid-nineteenth century by James's father, William Beale. The firm looked after the affairs of the Colmore estate in the Newhall area of Birmingham, but also specialised in railway work, which proved enormously profitable. The connection seems to have first been established by James's grandfather, another William Beale, who became a director of the Birmingham & Derby Railway in 1835. William's son, Samuel, was even more deeply involved in the railways, as an ironmaster supplying track to the railway companies, MP for the railway town of Derby and chairman of the Midland Railway from 1858 to 1864.

The Midland Railway, based in Derby, was created by the 'Railway King', George Hudson, during the railway mania of the mid-1840s. Through amalgamation and ruthless competition, it grew to control almost half of the railways in England by 1846. But for the next twenty years the ultimate prize, a London terminus, eluded the company. To achieve this, complex Bills had to be framed and steered through Parliament, often against intense opposition from rival companies. Land also had to be bought in north London and along the line of the new route. Good legal advice was absolutely essential, and James Beale provided it. His *Times* obituary recorded that 'as a Parliamentary agent no man had greater experience'.

The Midland Railway's long campaign finally ended in triumph with the opening of W. H. Barlow's great iron and glass train shed at St Pancras in 1868. The gigantic 240-feet span roof, cast by the Butterley Co. of Derbyshire, was at that time the

James Beale; by William Nicholson, 1905 (Inner Hall)

St Pancras from the Pentonville Road; by John O'Connor, 1884 (Museum of London)

largest such structure in the world. Equally over-powering is the neo-Gothic Midland Grand Hotel that fronts the station. Built of Nottingham salmon-pink brick and Derbyshire granite by the most fashionable architect of the day, Sir George Gilbert Scott, between 1868 and 1874, it announced in no uncertain fashion that the Midland Railway had arrived in London.

As the Midland Railway prospered and grew, so did Beale & Co. Negotiations over the London terminus had brought a great deal of work in the capital, and so the firm decided to open a London office, which James Beale was chosen to run. In 1870 he married Margaret Field, a member of another leading Nonconformist family in Birmingham, which proudly traced its ancestry back to Oliver Cromwell. The Beales set up home near St Pancras in Gordon Square, where their first four children, who arrived between 1871 and 1875, were born. In 1874 the eldest, Amy, was given the rocking horse now at Standen as a reward for having learnt her

alphabet; she called it Dobbin. Some time between 1875 and 1879, when their fifth child, Dorothy, was born, the family moved to the more salubrious surroundings of Kensington in west London. They chose a substantial detached villa, No. 32 Holland Park, which was part of an ambitious development put up by William and Francis Radford in the early 1860s on the Holland estate. This three-storey stucco house, with sizeable attic and basement, is now divided into flats, but it is not difficult to imagine it buzzing with Beale family life. When the 1881 census was taken, the household consisted of James and Margaret, their six children, a visitor (Margaret's mother, Sarah Field), a cook, parlour-maid, housemaid, kitchenmaid and two nursemaids (the two youngest children were then both under three). Like Philip Webb, James Beale enjoyed riding, and the large coach-house and stables in the mews behind the house must have been an additional attraction. From here it was a pleasant ride across the parks every day to his office in Great George Street in Westminster.

Holland Park very quickly became a fashionable address. The Beales' neighbours included a mixture of old and new money: the 4th Marquess of Londonderry, the Maharajah of Lahore, Sir William Fairbairn, the engineer and collector of modern pictures, and the cotton merchant Benjamin Whitworth MP. Directly across the street, at No. 1 Holland Park, lived the financier Alexander Ionides, a member of a remarkable family of Anglo-Greek patrons and collectors. In 1870 Ionides commissioned Thomas Jeckyll to build a billiard-room on to the house in the fashionable Japanese style. In 1880 the house was entirely redecorated by Morris & Co., which supplied large Hammersmith carpets, embroidered curtains and table covers, re-upholstered chairs and Morris wallpapers. Webb's chief assistant George Jack designed the dining-room table. Webb himself was involved in the decoration, and he also made additions to the home of Alexander's brother Constantine, just round the corner at 8 Holland Villas Road. Constantine's outstanding collection of modern French and British pictures is now in the Victoria & Albert Museum. Together these two houses became a showplace for the work of the Morris company, and it is tempting to suppose that the Beales may have first encountered it here. We know frustratingly little about James Beale's taste, but Margaret had strong artistic inclinations, and it would be surprising if she had not ordered Morris & Co. wallpapers to decorate 32 Holland Park.

In 1891 James Beale turned 50, he had seven children aged between five and nineteen, and he had made his fortune. Since Tudor times, successful lawyers have turned their fees into country houses. The reasons have been various. Soames Forsyte, the epitome of the wealthy late Victorian London solicitor memorably portrayed in John Galsworthy's *The Man of Property* (1906), builds Robin Hill in Surrey in an ultimately disastrous attempt to capture his wife's love. More prosaically, James Beale wanted somewhere to spend weekends with his family, play golf, and, ultimately, to retire. There should be land with the house over which to ride and shoot, but he had no need of a substantial estate in the old sense. What had in past centuries provided the wealth to build such houses, would, in the depressed agricultural conditions of the 1890s, simply have been a financial drain. It was to be a house in the country rather than a traditional country house.

Beale's father had bought himself a country house near Dolgellau in north Wales, Bryntirion, but he needed somewhere much nearer to his place of work. In the 1890s south-west Surrey and the Sussex Weald were the favoured spots for professional men from London looking for a country home. When the branch line from Oxted to East Grinstead opened in 1884, that area became within easy reach of London. So in 1890 he bought Great

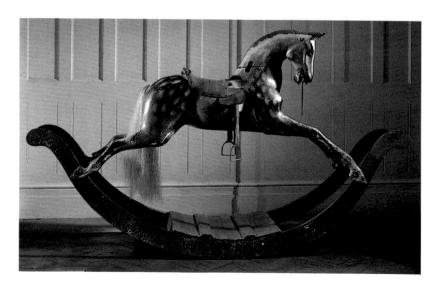

Dobbin, the rocking horse given to Amy Beale in 1874 as a reward for having learnt her alphabet. It now stands in the Billiard Room

Hollybush, Standen and Stone farms, in a picturesque setting among the rolling, wooded hills of the Sussex Weald to the south of East Grinstead.

But who should build the Beales' new house? If they had not seen Webb's work at the homes of Alexander and Constantine Ionides, they would have been introduced to it by the art-loving Alexander family in nearby Campden Hill or by the Queen's dentist, Sir John Tomes, who was also a friend and whose house, Upwood Gorse at Caterham in Surrey, had been built by Webb in 1873. There were several other Webb houses in the Holland Park neighbourhood for the Beales to consider, notably 1 (now 14) Holland Park Road,

designed in 1864 for Val Prinsep, and 1 Palace Green, commissioned in 1867 by George Howard, the young aesthete and heir of the 8th Earl of Carlisle. The Beales did not entertain on a lavish scale, so grand reception rooms were not required. The plain decoration and essential modesty of Webb's later houses must have appealed to a sober Unitarian like James Beale, whose aesthetic sense may have been influenced by worshipping in the austere interior of the Old Meeting House in Birmingham. Webb's reputation for building houses that did not go over budget or let in the rain must also have counted high with a careful lawyer like Beale. It was clear: Webb was the man.

Margaret Beale was an expert needlewoman and in William Nicholson's portrait of 1905 (in the Staircase Hall) is shown knitting

BEALE FAMILY TREE

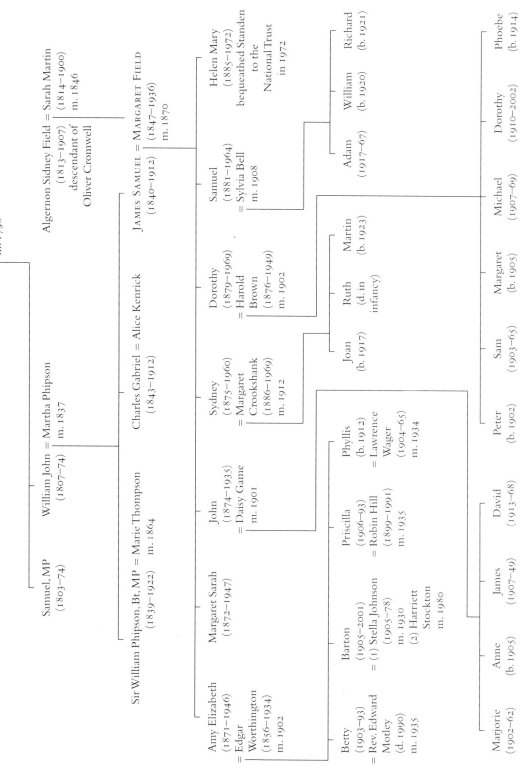

William Beale = Sarah Bailey
(1770–1848)   (d. 1822, aged 50)
m. 1796

Samuel, MP
(1803–74)

William John = Martha Phipson
(1807–74)   m. 1837

Algernon Sidney Field = Sarah Martin
(1813–1907)   (1814–1900)
descendant of   m. 1846
Oliver Cromwell

Charles Gabriel = Alice Kenrick
(1843–1912)   (1856–1934)

James Samuel = Margaret Field
(1840–1912)   (1847–1936)
m. 1870

Helen Mary
(1885–1972)
bequeathed Standen
to the
National Trust
in 1972

Sir William Phipson, Bt, MP = Marie Thompson
(1839–1922)   m. 1864

Amy Elizabeth
(1871–1946)
= Edgar
Worthington
(1856–1934)
m. 1902

Margaret Sarah
(1872–1947)

John
(1874–1935)
= Daisy Game
m. 1901

Sydney
(1875–1960)
= Margaret
Crookshank
(1886–1969)
m. 1912

Dorothy
(1879–1969)
= Harold
Brown
(1876–1949)
m. 1902

Samuel
(1881–1964)
= Sylvia Bell
m. 1908

Adam
(1917–67)

William
(b. 1920)

Richard
(b. 1921)

Betty
(1903–93)
= Rev. Edward
Motley
(d. 1990)
m. 1935

Barton
(1905–2001)
= (1) Stella Johnson
(1905–78)
m. 1930
(2) Harriett
Stockton
m. 1980

Priscilla
(1906–93)
= Robin Hill
(1899–1991)
m. 1935

Phyllis
(b. 1912)
= Lawrence
Wager
(1904–65)
m. 1934

Joan
(b. 1917)

Ruth
(d. in
infancy)

Martin
(b. 1923)

Marjorie
(1902–62)

Anne
(b. 1905)

James
(1907–49)

David
(1913–68)

Peter
(b. 1902)

Sam
(1903–65)

Margaret
(b. 1905)

Michael
(1907–69)

Dorothy
(1910–2002)

Phoebe
(b. 1914)

CHAPTER THREE

THE HOUSE

The whole of the work is to be done with the best *materials and workmanship of their several kinds . . . The* term best *means strictly what is implied thereby notwithstanding any other trade acceptance.*

From Webb's specification for Standen

On 11 April 1891 Philip Webb paid his first visit to the site with James and Margaret Beale. The attractions of the setting were obvious: a Wealden hillside looking south over a gentle valley (the bottom of which is now filled by Weirwood reservoir) towards Ashdown Forest. The site had already been levelled by G. B. Simpson, whom the Beales had commissioned to design the garden, but Webb managed to persuade them to choose a slightly different position nestling further into the slope. As at Clouds, there was a number of old farm buildings nearby. An earlier Victorian architect would simply have demolished them and used the rubble in the foundations of the new house. But that was never Webb's way. His first proposal was that 'the sounder part of the farm buildings should be kept standing, namely the barn, which has a good roof, only wooden walls wanting serious repair.' The barn was therefore included on his initial block plan for the new house, drawn up on 8 May. After a further visit, on 4 July, he had second thoughts, and decided that all the old buildings could be saved, including the Hollybush farmhouse. This farmhouse, dating in its earliest parts from about 1450, formed part of the service range of a large medieval manor house. It is a particularly attractive example of the Wealden vernacular, its walls hung with 'fish-scale' red tiles, the roof covered in massive slabs of Horsham sandstone speckled with lichen and moss; small panes fill the casement windows. It became integral to Webb's design, forming, with the old barn, the west and north sides of a spacious grassy area marked on the first plans as 'the House Green'

and now known as Goose Green. This has something of the flavour of a traditional village green and provides a typically understated introduction to the main house, which is connected to the southern end of the farmhouse by a covered archway. The service wing of the new house, which forms the south side of Goose Green, is much lower and simpler than the family block, to match the scale and mood of the older buildings. From the first, Webb's plans indicated the positions of an old walnut tree and yew tree. He was concerned to preserve ancient natural features of the landscape just as much as buildings.

Webb's evolving conception of Standen can be followed in detail through his meticulously numbered, dated and annotated drawings. The first plans envisaged the main block, containing the family rooms, facing south over the valley, with the lower servants' wing running at right angles from its north-east corner in a zig-zag north and east. The principal ground-floor rooms were laid out symmetrically on the south side of the house to take best advantage of the views and the light. On the early plans, L-shaped, bay-windowed dining- and drawing-rooms mirrored one another, with a square library between. A broad, straight corridor ran east–west down the spine of the house, connecting and on axis with the conservatory. The northern portion of the ground floor was occupied by a billiard-room (originally top-lit and detached from the main block), a secondary staircase, a business-room, an entrance porch and vestibule, a separate large entrance hall, and the main staircase. Projecting beyond the east end of the main block, forming the angle with the servants' wing was a morning-room, so placed as to get the best of the morning sun.

As happened quite often, Webb's initial scheme proved too expensive for his clients. Although Webb was unwilling to compromise on aesthetic

The south, garden front

*The fifteenth-century tile-hung Hollybush farmhouse, with,
to the left, Webb's entrance gateway and service wing*

grounds, he was quite prepared to give ground on practical matters and to save money, so long as there was no skimping with the materials used. The library was dispensed with; the dining-room was turned through 90°; the central corridor shrank and became more meandering; the servants' wing was shortened, and finally, in August 1891, the square entrance hall was absorbed into the vestibule, and the secondary staircase moved to the east corridor. By plan 9A and 8 September 1891 the plan as built was virtually agreed on.

On 7 November Webb paid his fourth visit to Standen, and pegged out the extent of the house on the ground. The next six months were spent producing the contract drawings. In June 1892 he drew up the detailed specification for all those who would be involved in constructing Standen: the builder, bricklayer, stonemason, tiler, carpenter, joiner, blacksmith, bellhanger, plasterer, plumber, glazier and painter. Together with the working drawings, which covered every element of the building, it left no doubt about what Webb wanted, and the high standards he demanded. He always

paid particular care in choosing the builder and craftsmen, preferring local men if their work came up to scratch. For Standen the builder selected was Peter Peters, of Horsham, the clerk of works a no-nonsense Yorkshireman, John Hardy, who also worked for Webb at Forthampton Court in Gloucestershire. The contract was signed in October 1892; work could now begin.

The old Hollybush farmhouse determined not only the siting of the new house, but also the traditional materials from which it was built. The specification noted that the external brickwork should be of 'well burned handmade red facing bricks from the Keymer yards . . . but *not* all of one color, occasional grey headers [bricks laid end on] and heat burred [vitrified] bricks to be mixed with the rest.' Concerned that, even with an admixture of darker bricks, the colour of the red Keymers might be too intense, he suggested as an alternative facing using local yellow-grey stock bricks from Horsham, reserving rubbed red Keymer brick for the detailing of the windows. This was the solution he finally settled on. Darker stocks were set aside to create chequer patterns, but they were to be used sparingly, avoiding the harsh contrasts that had discredited Butterfield's 'streaky bacon' style of polychrome brickwork. The bricks were to be laid in traditional English bond in mortar composed three parts of 'good clean local sand' to one part 'best Dorking lime'.

The specification also notes, 'If it is found that stone of satisfactory character and quality can be quarried at the west end of the site, this is to be used.' The stone, a creamy sandstone stained with iron mould, was satisfactory and quarrying began:

As soon as the quarried stone is sufficiently dry it is to be worked at once. All the facing stone is to be squared to beds and joints. The work for facing is to be done by axe, pick or broad chisel or all three according to circumstances. And the finished quality of the facing is to be of the kind shown in some old walling at the back of 'The Ship Inn', East Grinstead.

More impervious grey Portland stone was chosen for the window sills and those other parts most vulnerable to water and frost damage.

Clay tiles, whether pegged to roofs or hung from walls, are among the glories of Wealden architecture, and Webb used them extensively and with considerable subtlety at Standen. In contrast to the decorative 'fishscale' hanging tiles of the old farmhouse, he specified plain, handmade tiles; these have a variety of colour, texture and shape that machine-made tiles can never match. Webb might have liked to use Horsham stone on the roof, but the huge area and steep pitch of the main roof would never have supported their weight; expense also ruled them out. So he had to employ clay tiles again, laid in straw and fixed with fir pegs. After rain, roof-tiles hold water longer than vertical wall-tiles, encouraging lichen to grow, and they gradually lose the original brilliant red colour that hanging tiles always retain. This is only one way in which the English weather adds to the patina of a traditionally built house like Standen.

The weather-boarding in the gable ends was

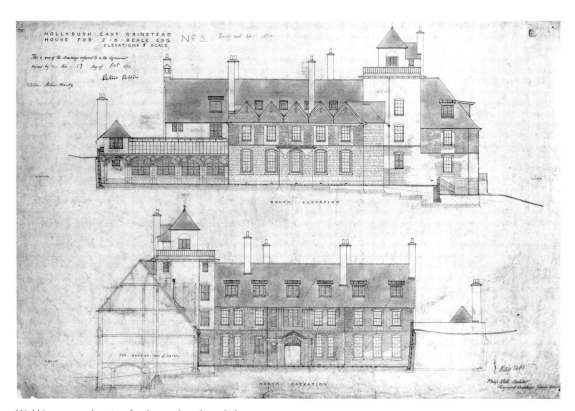

Webb's contract drawing for the north and south fronts

made of oak, fixed to fir studs and deal brackets. It was not painted, the practice with the smarter eighteenth-century houses, but, as at Penshurst, left to weather a beautiful dark grey. The sash-windows are of deal, while a tougher material, oak, was once again chosen for the vulnerable sills.

Roughcast is not native to the Sussex area, but is one of the oldest types of render and has always been associated with the more humble vernacular buildings. Webb used it at Standen for primarily practical reasons. He was concerned that the very exposed site might lead to water penetration of the upper levels of the brickwork in bad weather, and so he decided to protect the brick tower with an additional coating of roughcast made from lime, small broken stones, river pebbles and Russian tallow, and limewashed.

At Standen practicality determined the plan, and the existing buildings determined the materials used. Only once the plans had been agreed, did Webb discuss the elevations he had in mind with his clients. (He did not feel the need to produce enticing perspectives of the sort Norman Shaw was so skilled at devising.) Although much was therefore predetermined, the way Webb organised the exterior was extremely complex and personal, owing little to historical precedent, as becomes clear if one analyses the main fronts.

Each storey of the projecting, five-bay block at the centre of the garden front is treated in a different way. The walling of the ground floor, which contains the Dining Room and Drawing Room, is ashlar stone, laid in level, but unequal courses, very finely jointed. The windows (six panes by three, of the highest quality picture-glass) are Webb's favourite round-headed sashes. The frames were painted a 'parchment' white, to avoid an abrupt contrast with the recessed rubbed red-brick window surrounds. The central bay projects still further to provide a snug alcove in the Drawing Room, with views in three directions over the garden, and is shaded by a little canopy springing from stone corbels of a kind found in many of the bedrooms supporting the ceiling joists. The first floor is tile-hung. The window surrounds are again red brick, but here they project and are rather wider, and the windows themselves are square-headed, four panes

by three. The overhanging second floor, which offers shade to the bedrooms beneath, consists of a row of linked weather-boarded gable ends. Webb was very fond of this motif, for which there are many precedents, most famously the south-east front of Knole (1603–8), not far off in Kent. It creates a zig-zag rhythm that contrasts attractively with the plain expanse of tiled roof behind, which covers the bulk of the family block. The roof itself is only interrupted by little casement dormer windows between each gable end and by the tall chimneys of stock brick. Butterfield, Devey and Shaw had all enjoyed arranging tall chimneys against tiled roofs. It was characteristic of Webb that he should have reduced the idea to its essentials by designing absolutely plain chimneystacks.

The Red House had featured a miniature spire and Webb tried to include a tower of some sort in most of his later buildings. A tower was needed at Standen to hold two large water tanks, because, when first built, the house was entirely dependent for water on a windmill that pumped supplies up from the bottom of the valley. But the tower also provided a viewing platform and served as the central dominating element in Webb's composition, linking the family block with the servants' wing. It also acts as a foil for the long low Conservatory at the west end of the south front. Both the tower and the summer-house adjoining the Conservatory are topped by playful little belvederes with 'Sussex cap' roofs. By the 1890s conservatories were a common addition to country houses, but few were integrated so successfully into the overall design.

The north, entrance front has a completely different atmosphere, as it forms one side of an enclosed courtyard. It seems more private, but also more formal, with much less play of contrasting materials and shapes. Brick predominates and did so to an even greater extent before the stone bay window was added to the right of the entrance. The windows are placed awkwardly close together, probably because Webb's main concern was to provide the maximum window area on the darker, north side of the house. The broad stone hood over the porch is almost a pediment – the closest that Webb comes to classical detail at Standen. The servants' range to the left is less formal, with

The Dining Room windows on the east front have Webb's favourite round-headed sash frames. The window sills and little corbel are of Portland stone; the walling is a creamy sandstone quarried on the site. Webb used rubbed red Keymer bricks for the window surrounds and stock brick for the rest

weather-boarding and a lower and more varied roofline, but it was in no way to be seen as inferior.

All attempt at symmetry was abandoned in the east front, but it still contains some carefully considered groupings. The east end of the Dining Room is largely faced in stone, but the pair of tall narrow windows is placed within a recessed panel infilled with red brick, though with corbelled arches in stone above. The single dressing-room window above is centred on them, beneath a larger stone arch echoing those below.

Webb paid just as much attention to the design and fitting out of the interior. Visitors were welcomed into the modest Porch, simply panelled in

unpainted oak. Many of the other principal rooms are panelled up to picture-rail height. In the Drawing Room, Billiard Room, Staircase (and, after 1898, the Hall) the panelling was painted white, as at Clouds, but in the Dining Room a beautiful blue-green shade was chosen. Although the panelling is of the utmost simplicity, it was almost all designed by Webb himself down to the last bead and fillet.

Having left their hats and coats with the butler in the little room to the left, visitors turned right into the Hall, which Webb placed to one side to prevent draughts. Here, on a cold day, they could warm their hands at a substantial fireplace. Webb agreed with his disciple Lethaby that 'Notwithstanding all the names, there are only two modern styles of architecture: one in which the chimneys smoke, and the other in which they do not.' To ensure that Standen's chimneys fell into the second category, Webb inserted flue grilles above many of them. On the ground floor he also hung the doors to open away from the fireplaces, to prevent draughts blowing smoke out into the room. The open fires were supplemented from the start by a measure of central heating supplied by Longden's.

The chimney-pieces themselves deserve attention. No two in the house are the same, and they show Webb at his most creative and unrestrained. The huge keystone and semi-circular arch of the Hall chimney-piece seem to have escaped from a baroque palace by Vanbrugh, and the mantel has been split into three, with a York stone apron below. The overmantels are, for the most part, merely extensions of the surrounding panelling. However, above Webb's favourite lozenge pattern in the Dining Room is a panel of more elaborate fretwork decoration, which recalls, in a simplified form, his plasterwork at Clouds. (The plasterwork at Standen is not decorated in any way.)

The Drawing Room and Dining Room fireplaces have, in addition, repoussé metal cheeks also designed by Webb. Like Morris's wallpapers, their decoration is based on plant forms, but those in the Dining Room are abstracted to a degree that Morris would never have contemplated. They were made by John Pearson, the senior metalworker in C.R. Ashbee's Guild of Handicraft when it was founded in 1888, and a specialist in this kind of repoussé work, other examples of which can be seen around the house. Pearson also made the matching fender and fire-irons; those in the Drawing Room have now, alas, gone.

From the Hall one can walk straight across into the Billiard Room. Onlookers could enjoy the game from the comfortable raised sofa in the arched niche at the far end of the room. The Beales wanted more room for similar sociable seating, and so in 1898 Webb, somewhat reluctantly, created a further inglenook by moving the corner fireplace and taking in part of the adjacent west corridor. The panelling and the bookshelves were also added, in

Webb's design for the repoussé metal cheeks of the Dining Room fireplace

1907, probably by George Jack, perhaps to Webb's design. The parquet flooring of 'Daffy's Immovable Acme 1½ Yellow Deal' woodblocks is, however, original. Oak floorboards were laid in the Dining Room and Drawing Room, deal in the upstairs bedrooms; those in the Larkspur Dressing Room were stained green, a colour previously avoided for such rooms, as early pigments usually contained arsenic. York stone and red tiles were chosen for the Servants' Corridor, which was likely to receive the most wear. Mrs Beale was worried about the cost of the plain nine-inch-square red tiles that Webb proposed to use in the Conservatory, but he was convinced that they would be 'much better than any "fancy" ones, and would be sure to agree with the flowers'. He went on:

If you should prefer it, I could lay the floor with York stone, but it would be rather more costly than the tiles, and would look colder. I would still recommend the plain red tiles. Any kind of glazed tile is disagreeable to walk upon, and more so from the nails in country shoes.

The delicate cast-iron frame of the Conservatory roof was based on that Webb had designed in 1883 for the top-lit central hall of Bell Brothers' offices in Middlesbrough. The Conservatory epitomises Webb's fascination in his later work with creating light-filled interiors. Not only is it a pleasant spot on a sunny afternoon, but the bull's-eye windows (a feature of the Red House) borrow light from it to illuminate what had originally been part of the central corridor. From the first, Standen was also lit by electricity generated by a donkey engine in a shed beside the old barn. The original light-fittings still survive in most of the rooms. In the Drawing Room they take the form of large copper sconces fixed to the wall above the picture rail, each featuring a repoussé sunflower to match the fireplace cheeks. From the stamen of the sunflower projects a metal bracket from which the glass-shaded bulb hangs. Again, Webb provided the design for Pearson to carry out, but in this case Webb allowed him a little freedom in interpreting the motif. In a letter to Mrs Beale, Webb warned, 'The copper plates should *not* be scoured, but only occasionally rubbed with wash leather.' Most of the

One of the copper Drawing Room light-fittings, which were designed by Webb and made by John Pearson

other light-fittings, standard and table lamps were made by W. A. S. Benson, a protégé of Morris who became managing director of Morris & Co. after the founder's death in 1896. He also ran a shop in Bond Street specialising in 'artistic' metalwork.

Webb designed all the fitted dressers, cupboards and shelving in which Standen abounds, and which he sited with particular care to meet the needs of both family and staff. Trays of food on their way to the Dining Room could be placed in the lobby outside, on a shelf kept warm by the radiator below it. From there they could be transferred to the dressers which line the Dining Room alcove. A recessed dresser with flanking cupboards in the corridor leading to the Morning Room served a similar purpose.

Many of the bedrooms have fitted wardrobes, again designed by Webb. In August 1893 he asked Amy Beale where she would like him to put the wardrobe in her room, the Larkspur Bedroom. Eventually, they settled on the present position to the left of the fireplace, and he made sure to include a full-length mirror in the wardrobe door. Webb also indicated on the plans his suggested positions for the beds, 'sizes as for a tallish family'. For modesty and draught prevention, the doors were hung to open away from the beds.

The bedrooms (twelve on the first floor for the family and their guests, nine on the second for the servants and the younger children) were served by only two bathrooms, with Cliff's patent full-size porcelain baths and Newman nickel-plated fittings. The old-fashioned Webb still expected most people to bathe in hip-baths in their own rooms. There was a rather more generous provision of seven lavatories, fed by 'Deluge' patent galvanised iron cisterns. Good plumbing was an obsession with Webb; indeed the only professional body to which he belonged was the Institute of Sanitary Engineers.

The servants' wing was laid out and fitted up with just as much care as the rest. From the Butler's Pantry the butler could keep an eye on all the comings and goings down the Servants' Corridor, but also look out on to the entrance courtyard for arriving visitors. Next to it is the Servants' Hall which enjoys the best light in the evening, when the servants might expect to have a little time for relaxation. The Kitchen across the corridor opposite was fitted with a range by Smith & Wellstood Ltd of London and a sizeable dresser; its windows looked north for the sake of coolness. Leading off it are the Scullery, Cook's Pantry and two larders, which together form one prong of a U-shaped range laid out around an arcaded kitchen courtyard. The other prong takes in the Cook's Store, the Brushing Room, two coal bunkers, and separate storerooms for boots and knives, empty bottles and wood. Casks of beer could be lowered directly into the cellars below through a trapdoor in the courtyard. The servants' quarters at Standen might not be as elaborate as in the grander Victorian country houses, but they were still substantial.

In August 1894 Webb completed work on Standen. The total cost was £18,065, his fee £820. The Beales could now begin the task of decorating and furnishing their new country home.

CHAPTER FOUR

THE FURNISHINGS

Have nothing in your houses that you do not know to be useful or believe to be beautiful.

William Morris

If the Beales had not already employed Morris & Co. to decorate 32 Holland Park, then Webb would certainly have recommended that they did so at Standen. As a result, the house is now one of the finest surviving examples of the Morris company's work in all its variety of pattern, colour and texture – from printed wallpapers and chintzes to handstitched embroidery, from stamped velvet to lampas, carpets and tapestries.

WALLPAPERS

The first priority was wallpaper, which, unlike the fabrics and furniture, was supplied entirely by Morris & Co. Morris's first wallpaper design, 'Trellis', had been manufactured in 1864. Drawing inspiration from the old varieties of native plants that were grown in the Red House garden, and rejecting the twee literalism of early Victorian papers, Morris demonstrated an extraordinary talent for translating the rhythms of natural forms into repeating two-dimensional patterns. He was less good with animals, so it was Webb, who loved sketching birds, who contributed the birds which cling to the trellis. By 1894 Morris and his chief assistant, J.H.Dearle, had designed at least 50 patterns, which were hand-printed from wooden blocks by Jeffrey & Co. of Islington. This was a laborious and essentially uncreative process, but it enabled Morris to use slower-drying, richer inks than was possible with wallpapers machine-printed from engraved rollers – the standard Victorian technique.

Morris papers were used quite sparingly in the principal ground-floor rooms at Standen, and the Beales seem to have preferred the firm's earlier, less ornate designs, perhaps under the influence of Webb. There are no papers in the Porch, Hall, Dining Room and Morning Room, where panelling or patterned textiles predominate, and in the Billiard Room 'Pomegranate' is now restricted to the 1898 alcove. 'Sunflower' covers all but the east wall of the Drawing Room, matching Pearson's sunflower metalwork, but one of the less assertive colour-ways was chosen. Papers are much more obvious in the passages: 'Trellis' in the Morning Room and Conservatory Corridors (an appropriate introduction to the Conservatory), and 'Bachelor's Button' in the Staircase Hall, up the stairs, and along the Bedroom Corridor, where it was hung above panelling and varnished as a protection against scuffing. In the first-floor bedrooms Morris wallpapers dominate. However, care was taken to choose papers without elaborate patterns for the bedrooms. As the manual on home decoration produced by Agnes and Rhoda Garrett (see below) recommends:

Select a paper that has an all-overish pattern that cannot be tortured into geometrical figures by the occupant of the chamber, who, especially in hours of sickness, is well-nigh driven to distraction by counting over and over again the dots and lines and diamonds which dance with endless repetition before his aching eyes.

In 1906, while the Beales were on a round-the-world holiday, the Morris company repaired and replaced many of the Standen wallpapers, supplying 'Looptrail' and 'Merton' for the bedrooms of the Beales' two unmarried sons, 'Grafton' for the Day

(Opposite) 'Bachelor's Button' wallpaper, designed by William Morris in 1892. It hangs in the Staircase Hall and Bedroom Corridor, and was varnished by the Beales to protect it from damage

'Powdered' wallpaper, designed by Morris in 1874, is typical of the designs chosen for the Standen bedrooms

Nursery, and 'Oak Tree' for the Servants' Hall. Repapering has occasionally been necessary since, but in most cases the desired effect has not been lost, as replacements, hand-printed from Morris's original, if somewhat worn, blocks, were still available.

TEXTILES

William Morris first became interested in textile design through the medium of embroidery. His earliest, rather faltering efforts to master this technique were produced at Red Lion Square in 1857. Once he had taught his wife Janey and her sister Elizabeth to embroider, he concentrated on producing designs from which they could make woollen hangings for the Red House. His daughter May subsequently became a highly skilled maker and designer of embroideries. Margaret Beale was also an exceptionally fine needlewoman, a member of that generation of upper middle-class women who helped to revive fine embroidery in Britain and to

found the Royal School of Art Needlework in 1872. In the late 1870s she embroidered one of Morris's finest early hangings, which is now in the Victoria & Albert Museum, together with Morris's working drawing. It forms a repeating pattern of lotus blossom worked in silks, in shades of peach and brown, on a dark blue ground. Unlike block-printed or woven textiles, there is no technical reason why embroidery should employ a repeating design, but Morris obviously felt happier working within such a grid.

Margaret Beale passed on her skills to her daughters, and in particular Maggie, who studied Fine Art at the Slade and in Paris, and designed her own embroidered cushion covers, bedspreads and stool-tops, based, in best Morris tradition, on flowers in the Standen garden. She also produced patterns for family and friends to embroider, and span her own yarn. Her studio was initially in the Westbourne Room, which had the necessary steady north light. There was also a sewing-room on the second floor, which was used by the lady's maid Clara Smith, who was another expert needlewoman. Together, the Standen women embroidered in silk the very fine version of Morris's 'Artichoke' design which now hangs in the North Bedroom. The design was originally commissioned by Ada Godman for Smeaton Manor in Yorkshire, which had been built by Philip Webb for the Godmans in 1876–7. Morris delivered the pattern in 1877, but the large and intricate panels took Ada Godman many years to complete, working in wool on a linen backing.

In later years Morris became less interested in producing patterns specifically for embroidery, and so many of his designs for other media were adapted for this purpose. The cushion covers in the Drawing Room embroidered by the Beales were based on his 'Trellis' and 'Pomegranate' wallpaper designs. The hanging in the Hall, also embroidered by Margaret Beale and her daughters, follows the pattern of 'Vine', a wallpaper designed by Morris in 1873.

About 1891 Dearle designed the 'Daffodil' chintz, 48¼ yards of which Margaret Beale ordered in April 1894, together with a plain yellow lining, to hang against the Morning Room walls. 'Daffodil' is one of many Morris printed textiles used in different ways by the Beales at Standen. It was printed by hand from wooden blocks (like the Morris papers) at Merton Abbey in Surrey, the factory founded by Morris in 1881 to produce textiles to the high standards he demanded. Unhappy with the aniline dyes used in most Victorian fabrics, which were both garish and fugitive, Morris experimented to rediscover the recipes for traditional vegetable pigments. (For several years his hands were bright blue, so stained had they become in the vats of woad dye.) Finding the right colour was of particular importance for Morris hanging textiles, because the folds of the material made the pattern less easy to read than was the case with wallpapers, which were generally printed in many more colour-ways. The narrow, nine-inch horizontal repeat of the 'Daffodil' pattern compensates for this to a certain extent. (The present hanging in the Morning Room is a modern, not altogether faithful, reproduction.)

Margaret Beale also ordered substantial quantities of 'African Marigold' and 'Severn' chintzes in 1894, presumably to be used as hangings and curtains in other rooms; during the 1906 redecoration, there were further orders of 4½ pairs of curtains of 'Cray' lined with the smaller-repeat 'Borage' for the east corridor, plus lesser amounts of the 'Strawberry Thief' and 'Honeysuckle' patterns (the Morris firm's telegraph address was 'Honeysuckle, London'). Morris printed cotton fabrics are now to be seen at Standen mainly in the curtains: 'Compton' in the Billiard Room, 'Scroll' (which was adapted from the background of the 'Powdered' wallpaper, seen in the North Bedroom) in the Larkspur Dressing Room, 'Tulip' in the Willow Bedroom, 'Lodden' in the North Bedroom.

Printed cottons had been used since the eight-

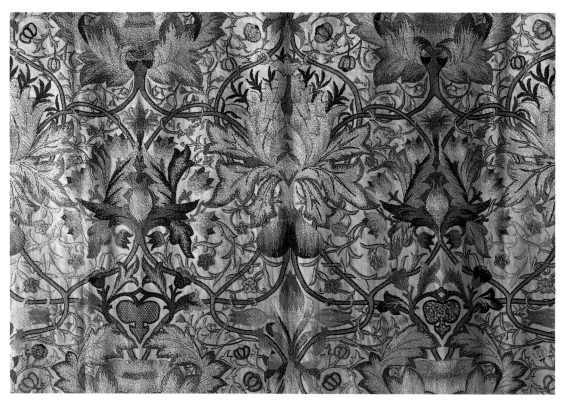

'Artichoke', designed by Morris and embroidered by Margaret Beale and her daughters about 1896 (North Bedroom). Silk on linen ground

eenth century as loose covers for furniture, but Morris was one of the first to employ them widely for upholstery. The Morris & Co. catalogues produced after his death show the firm's furniture upholstered with a wide variety of chintzes; in 1894 the Beales chose pieces made up with 'Wandle', 'Tulip and Willow' and 'Lodden' patterns. More traditional for such upholstery was stamped velvet. This was hard-wearing and an important element in the 'Queen Anne' look. One of the first fabrics sold by Morris & Co., in 1871, was 'Utrecht Velvet', which was based on a seventeenth-century Dutch fabric and may have been bought in from the range of the Manchester furnishing firm J. Aldam Heaton & Co. There is a rather faded example of this design, which was stamped on to mohair plush material, on one of the armchairs in the Drawing Room. Standen also possesses a settee and set of chairs

'Wey' printed velveteen hanging, designed by Morris c.1883 (Hall)

upholstered with red 'Acorn' stamped silk velvet in very much better condition.

Morris did not recommend his woven fabrics for upholstery because they wore less well than printed cotton or velvet. However, they were in great demand for hangings and curtains, particularly among the more traditionally minded decorators, who had always appreciated the rich and more complex texture of woven stuffs. These were made mostly on power-driven Jacquard-looms, either at Merton Abbey or by outside contractors. Since the destruction of the punched cards used to programme these looms in 1940, they have become almost impossible to reproduce accurately. The 'Bird and Vine' and 'Peacock and Dragon' woven curtains in the Business Room and Dining Room respectively are both original to the house, and the latter is among the finest of all Morris's designs. Although inspired in both pattern and colour by Middle Eastern sources, it is, as Linda Parry notes, 'the closest he ever came to his early ideal of English medieval hangings'. Woven woollen double cloth 'Bird' and silk and cotton 'Tulip and Rose' hangings decorate the Conservatory Corridor and Drawing Room.

With its curtains, Morris & Co. supplied curtain rods and rings, 'steel bronzed' brass in the Drawing and Dining Room, cheaper plain brass for the less important rooms. The firm also installed cream Holland roller blinds to keep the rooms cool in summer and prevent damage to the fabrics from direct sunlight. For conservation reasons these have had to be replaced by dark blue blinds, which, even when raised, change the effect somewhat.

Spectacular carpets designed by Morris were one of the glories of 1 Holland Park and Clouds, but the Beales never commissioned anything as grand. In 1894 they ordered a few Kidderminster and Wilton carpets from the company, together with quantities of corticine, a form of linoleum very popular as a practical floor-covering in the late nineteenth century, for the lavatories and bathrooms. It was printed with a pattern of African marigolds growing through an arched trellis. Most of the carpets came from other sources: George P. and J. Baker, 'importers of Oriental goods', provided Turkish carpets for the Business Room ('Peacock Blue'),

'St Agnes' tapestry (Bedroom Corridor); the figure was designed by Burne-Jones (originally for stained glass), the foliage background by Morris

Morning Room ('Mosaic'), Dining Room ('Mignonette and Green' and 'Plain') and Drawing Room ('Camel'). There were also Persian rugs and carpets from Maple's, and Axminster, Ushak and Indian from Liberty's. During the 1906 redecoration Morris & Co. laid Patent Axminster rugs and runners with a mottled apricot and pink centre and patterned borders in the Inner Hall and on the half-landing, and up the main stairs, which survive in part and were woven in full during 2000. In the 1920s Dorothy Beale's husband, Harold, brought back a particularly fine Persian carpet from the Gulf, where he had been involved in much legal work for the oil companies, and it was laid in the Dining Room. The very grand hand-knotted Morris & Co. carpet in the Drawing Room, which was designed by J. H. Dearle, did not belong to the Beales, but has been introduced by the National Trust as an accompaniment to the other Morris furnishings.

Despite his love of medieval tapestries, Morris turned to this, the grandest of all the textile-weaving techniques, only in his later years, and he never devoted much time to it, perhaps because he was so uncomfortable designing figures. The firm seems to have supplied no tapestries to Standen, although some bills refer, rather vaguely, to woven wool textiles by this name. However, the *St Agnes* panel, acquired by Arthur Grogan and now hanging in the Bedroom Corridor, is a good example of the firm's tapestry work. The figure is based on a design originally produced by Burne-Jones for stained glass; the foliage background was added by Morris. The panel was originally woven in 1887, with a matching *St Cecilia*, for Sir Thomas Wardle, the Staffordshire fabric dyer and printer who had produced most of Morris's early textiles.

FURNITURE

Furniture-making was always a comparatively small part of the Morris & Co. business. It is not surprising, therefore, that the most important pieces at Standen should have been made by other firms. The furniture designed by Agnes Garrett and her cousin Rhoda was probably bought in the 1870s, and seems to have come down to Standen only after the London house was sold in 1912. The Garretts were remarkable members of a remarkable family of feminists. Agnes's sisters were Elizabeth Garrett Anderson, the first woman to qualify as a doctor in England, and Millicent Fawcett, the pioneer suffragist. Rhoda Garrett, who herself was to publish a lecture on *Electoral disabilities of women* in 1872, came down to London in 1867 and, with her cousin, joined the office of J. M. Brydon to train as an architect – a then unheard-of occupation for a woman. In the early 1870s the Garretts set up their own interior design firm together in Gower Street, offering 'artistic' furniture and furnishings in the increasingly popular Queen Anne style to a middle-

class public, whose appetite for more harmonious surroundings had been whetted by C. L. Eastlake's *Hints on Household Taste* (1868). In 1876 they published their own handbook of advice, *Suggestions for House Decoration in Painting, Woodwork and Furniture*, which went through at least six editions. Morris is not mentioned by name, but they were undoubtedly influenced by his ideas: 'Trellis' wallpaper appears in their suggested decoration for a dining-room. Webb would have approved the principles of honesty and simplicity that lie at the heart of the Garretts' philosophy of decoration: 'Never go out of your way to make a thing or a material look like what it is not'; 'Do not go out of your way to hide the construction of your house or of any part of your furniture'; 'Always secure a considerable amount of plain neutral colour in your rooms'. The Beales certainly approved, as they bought a number of Garrett pieces, including a corner-cupboard now in the Morning Room, which was featured in *Suggestions*. The Garretts recommended such corner-cupboards where space was short, and included mirror glass as they thought it the best background for china.

The grandest furniture bought new for Standen was commissioned from Collinson & Lock. The firm was established in 1870, and made its name at the International Exhibition the following year, growing to become one of the most successful 'Art Furnishers' in Britain. From the start it employed leading architect-designers such as T. E. Collcutt and E. W. Godwin on substantial retainers. Collcutt, like Webb and Morris a pupil of G. E. Street, designed the bureau-cabinet in the Morning Room, which may have been made by Collinson & Lock. The chair in the Drawing Room bay window is a Godwin piece. From 1885 the firm employed Stephen Webb, a member of the Arts and Crafts Exhibition Society and no relation of Philip, as its chief designer. He specialised in creating rosewood cabinets with highly elaborate ivory inlay somewhat in the manner of Italian Renaissance grotesque

(Left and opposite) The Morning Room corner-cupboard, which was designed by Agnes and Rhoda Garrett. It was illustrated in the Garretts' Suggestions for House Decoration in Painting, Woodwork and Furniture *(1876)*

decoration. The cabinet between the windows in the Drawing Room is one of his designs. In 1896 the Beales also commissioned two major suites from Collinson & Lock: a bedroom suite in rosewood, inlaid with boxwood, consisting of wardrobe, dressing-table, washstand and pedestal cupboard, costing £294; and a simpler rosewood dressing-room suite containing the same elements plus a chest of drawers and costing £105. Both are still at Standen, distributed around the bedrooms and dressing-rooms. They must be among the last independent pieces produced by the firm, as it was taken over the following year by Gillow's of Lancaster.

The more workaday furniture came from a number of sources. S. & J. Jewell supplied a 'richly carved Spanish mahogany Chippendale' dining-table and sixteen 'Jacobean' dining-chairs, also of Spanish mahogany, which are still in the Dining Room. From Heal's the Beales bought simple brass bedsteads which were considered both more hygienic and easier to move than traditional wooden-framed models. Heal's also provided hair mattresses, goose-feather bolsters and down pillows, Maple's

the kitchen table and towel horses for the dressing-rooms and bathrooms.

Morris & Co. furniture was not totally forgotten. By the 1890s the firm had more or less given up selling the plain, heavy pieces that Webb had designed in its early days, to concentrate on more conservative and popular Georgian revival designs. The glass-fronted cabinet in the Drawing Room is typical: designed by George Jack, it was described in the Morris catalogue as 'of highest Sheraton finish'. Among the three settees the Beales bought from Morris & Co. was the 'Chippendale' model. Less directly imitative of the past is the 'Saville' easy chair in the Drawing Room, again designed by Jack, who succeeded Webb as the firm's principal furniture maker. In addition, Standen possesses the two most famous pieces of Morris furniture, which, appropriately enough, both have Sussex connections. What became known as the 'Morris' chair was, according to Warington Taylor, the business manager of the firm, based on 'a chair model which I saw with an old carpenter at Hurstmonceux, Sussex by name Ephraim Colman'. This armchair with button-backed cushions and adjustable back was sold from 1860 and the design became immensely popular in Britain and the USA, where it was serenaded by Bing Crosby:

I love your loving arms,
They hold a world of charms
A place to nestle when I am lonely
A cosy Morris chair
Oh, what a happy pair . . .

Even more successful was the 'Sussex' chair, which derived from traditional rush-seated chairs of ebonised wood found throughout the county. They were manufactured to many patterns by the Morris firm, and copied by every other major furniture company, as they had all the essential ingredients for success, being strong, light, comfortable, cheap to make and undatable. Those supplied to Standen by Maple's in 1894 cost only 9/6. Webb also seems to have incorporated vernacular chair design into the decoration of Standen, for the banisters on the main staircase curiously resemble a simplified version of the splat in a traditional Windsor chair.

CERAMICS

The Victorian and Edwardian art pottery at Standen was largely collected by the first administrator, Arthur Grogan (see Chapter Five), but it is still very much in keeping with the style and original contents of the house. The Victorian penchant for country-made crafts is admirably represented by the wares of Sir Edmund Elton and the Barnstaple potteries of Brannam, Lauder and Baron, which do not look out of place beside the Beales' fine Rockingham bone china tea-service, or indeed their Collinson & Lock furniture and Persian carpets. Dating mostly from between 1880 and 1912, a variety of wares is shown, but by far the most dominant are the collections of William De Morgan's lustre ware and Della Robbia majolica.

William De Morgan (1839–1917) established his pottery in 1869, initially for the production of enamel decorated tiles. He is best known, however, for his lustre decoration, early experiments with which he made on white blanks from other potteries. He was a good friend of William Morris, and Morris & Co. retailed many of his wares.

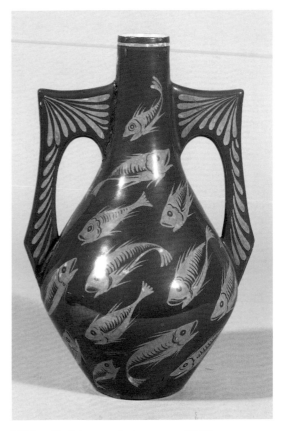

William De Morgan ruby lustre vase (Hall)

De Morgan's ceramic work covers five main periods and all are represented at Standen: his early beginnings in Fitzroy Square (1869–72) and Chelsea (1872–82); production of his own pottery close to Morris's Merton Abbey factory (1882–8); and his mature style at Sand's End, Fulham, firstly, in partnership with the architect Halsey Ricardo (1888–98) and, secondly, with his kilnmaster Iles and the Passenger brothers (1898–1907), both of whose work may be seen at Standen.

De Morgan effectively rediscovered the art of lustre decoration, popular in sixteenth-century Italy and prevalent as far back as ninth-century Persia, in which glazes were given a metallic or iridescent sheen by adding a thin film of a dissolved metal oxide in the final firing. His relentless experiments resulted in spectacular creations of ruby lustre (well represented in the Hall), and, later, two-tone lustres (for example, the charger in the Morning Room). Decorations featured designs from the Italian Renaissance, Iznik, Syrian and Persian styles, fantastical beasts, galleons, animals, fish, birds and floral subjects.

Other nineteenth-century lustre ware is from the Florentine pottery of Cantagalli, and from the area around Cannes on the French Riviera, in particular the work of Clément Massier at Golfe Juan, and Léon Castel at the Faiencerie du Mont Chevalier.

The Della Robbia Pottery, founded in 1894 at Birkenhead by the artist Harold Rathbone and the sculptor Conrad Dressler, took its name from the fifteenth-century family of Florentine sculptors in terracotta, and sought to produce majolica in the manner of the Italian Renaissance. The pottery had close connections with exponents of the Arts and Crafts movement and gained royal patronage, but was short-lived, closing in 1906. The characteristic crude sgraffito (incised) decorations in yellow and green glaze on a rough terracotta body are seen to good effect in the pieces throughout the house, and there are examples of the work of many of the main Della Robbia artists, including a coloured plaster relief of *Charity* by the painter and sculptor Robert Anning Bell on the top landing.

Della Robbia majolica charger, bearing the 'ship' mark of the firm (Morning Room)

William De Morgan late Fulham period (1898–1907) two-tone lustre charger (Morning Room)

The slipware of Sir Edmund Elton (1846–1920) is characterised by relief floral patterns set against shiny, dark streaked glazes on terracotta bodies. Elton's engineering expertise can be seen in the interesting shapes he chose for his ceramics. (He was an accomplished inventor, with many patents for gas-lighting and bicycles to his credit.) The pieces at Standen date from between 1890 and 1920. A comprehensive collection of Elton Ware can be seen at Clevedon Court in Somerset, Elton's home and now also the property of the National Trust.

Another important West Country centre for Victorian art pottery was Barnstaple in Devon, where the pottery of Charles Hubert Brannam (1855–1937), which is still operating, produced elaborate slip-decorated wares on classical and Victorian shapes. Brannam designers shown at Standen include James Dewdney, Frederick Braddon, Beauchamp Whimple and William Baron. Baron (1863–1937) went on to form his own pottery nearby in 1893, producing similar wares. Alexander Lauder (1836–1921), again represented here, also had a pottery in the Barnstaple area. Many of the Barnstaple wares were known as Barum Ware, after the Roman name for the town, and are marked as such.

CHAPTER FIVE

LIFE AT STANDEN

On entering the front door we met the special Standen aroma of dried rose petals, eucalyptus and mimosa, which survives in memory today.

Standen Memories

Standen was home to James and Margaret Beale and their seven children, Amy, Maggie, Jack, Sydney, Dorothy, Sam and Helen, from 1894 until 1901, when the children began marrying and moving away to set up their own homes. However, for the next 70 years Standen remained the focus of family life, to which the Beale children brought back their own numerous offspring for summer holidays and at Christmas. By 1914 there were already fourteen grandchildren and there were to be nineteen in all. The many Beale, Field, Kenrick and Chamberlain cousins were also welcome visitors. Standen was rarely empty.

James and Margaret's grandchildren have left a vivid account of life at Standen in the years before and after the First World War. The day began when housemaids brought up to their bedrooms copper jugs of hot water under huge tea-cosies. After they had washed, there was breakfast, either in the nursery, which had been created in 1901 by George Jack by knocking together a pair of the smaller bedrooms on the first floor; or, when they were older, with the adults in the Dining Room. It was a hearty meal, starting with porridge, and including a variety of hot dishes, scones, large cups of milk or coffee, and ending with peaches from the garden, when they were in season.

After breakfast the women moved to the Morning Room where they wrote letters, read the morning papers or chatted over their embroidery patterns. The men retired to the Billiard Room for a smoke and, later in the day, a game of snooker or

(Opposite) Phyllis Worthington on the red Standen trolley

billiards. The male atmosphere of the room was reinforced by the oars hanging over the bookcase: both Jack and Sam had been Cambridge Blues, and Sydney also rowed at Oxford. Despite the oars, and the university prints and Cromwell portraits on the walls, the Billiard Room was not an entirely adult male preserve. Helen became an expert billiards player and taught the game to those nephews and nieces who could be relied on not to tear the baize. The Drawing Room was not entered until after lunch by anyone but staff or flower arrangers. 'Doing the flowers' was a job often given to one of the grandchildren, using daffodils, sweet peas, chrysanthemums or carnations cut from the garden.

Lunch was taken in the Dining Room where the embroidered chairseats were often hidden by linen covers to protect them from wear and sunlight. The food at Standen was always good. The local butcher and grocer delivered to the back door regularly. Grapes, nectarines, melons and much else were grown in the glasshouses for the table. The white-tiled dairy, next to the farmhouse, made delicious butter and cream from the farm's herd. Much of the produce from the estate was also sent up in hampers to the Beales' various London homes. James's sister-in-law, Marie Beale, ensured that standards in the kitchen did not slip: she was a famous cook, whose *Wholesome Cookery* (1886) went through many editions. The food in the Servants' Hall was of an equally high standard – 'scrumptious', one ex-housemaid called it. The cook also kept a supply of pink creams to hand for grandchildren who ventured into the Kitchen. The young Beales had very healthy appetites. They once competed to see how much weight they could put on at one sitting. The record, measured on the scales in the Conservatory Corridor, was five pounds.

To his grandchildren James Beale, who retired

*The Beale children around the time Standen was built:
(from left to right) Maggie, Sam, Sydney, Jack, Dorothy,
Helen and Amy*

from Beale & Co. in the early twentieth century, was a rather remote figure, a kindly but austere Victorian paterfamilias, who was mainly seen at meal-times, when he would stand at the dresser expertly carving the joint. One of his chief retirement pleasures was a little gentle and inexpert golf. As his obituary in *The Times* records, 'He was president of the Royal Ashdown Forest Golf Club, a position he owed not so much to his skill in the game as to the fact that he was a prominent and highly respected resident in the neighbourhood of the course.' He continued to ride, keeping a sizeable string of horses in the stables built by Webb behind the Hollybush farmhouse. His grandchildren were often taken over to feed them carrots. Beale also

taught his children and grandchildren to shoot in the Standen woods and at Drumlamford, the Ayrshire estate of his elder brother, William.

After lunch Margaret Beale would read aloud to the grandchildren from her armchair by the fireplace in the Drawing Room. There was plenty to choose from the shelves in the Morning Room and Billiard Room: Robert Louis Stevenson, Walter Scott, Harrison Ainsworth and the stirring Victorian children's tales of G. A. Henty and his kind. As she read, silently omitting passages thought unsuitable for young ears, she would knit socks. The house rule, not always strictly observed, was 'no novels before lunch'.

On dry afternoons there was always the garden for the grandchildren to explore. They could play in the sand-pit on the top garden lawn with buckets and spades that were kept in a cupboard under the back stairs. In the same cupboard lived a little red trolley, on which succeeding generations of young Beales would race at high speed down the sloping main lawn. Here they also learnt to ride a bicycle, often ending up in an undignified heap among the rhododendrons at the bottom. They played at being savages, stalking through the shrubberies with spears made from bamboo canes. They sailed model boats on the rock garden pond or went blackberrying in the woods, bringing back laden baskets to be weighed in the Kitchen. On wet days they could always ride on Amy's old rocking horse in the nursery, or play in the tiny summer-house, up steps at the end of the Conservatory. The family story goes that in 1893 the youngest of the Beale children, Helen, then aged seven, asked Webb to build 'a little room' specially for her; he charged her sixpence. A door from the summer-house leads out on to a wide ledge above the Conservatory, which became a favourite refuge for the young. The braver grandchildren risked their necks sliding head first down the fire escape, a canvas tube suspended from the sewing-room window two floors above the Morning Room.

In the summer the family played tennis or croquet on the flat lawn below the house. On one special occasion there was a week-long festival of Morris dancing. When the weather was hot, tea was brought out to the summer-house by the croquet lawn. Otherwise it was taken in the Conservatory, or, if not warm enough there, then in the Hall. The Beales found the Hall, as first built, too small and dark for such tea parties. So in 1898 they asked Webb back to modify it. He added the stone bay window, which lengthened the room by nine and a half feet, and repainted the panelling, originally red, the present shade of white.

The Beales remained on friendly terms with Webb. In 1902 James's sister-in-law Alice presented a ceremonial mace designed by Webb to the new University of Birmingham. In the same year Webb retired, moving to Caxtons, a cottage in Worth ten miles west of Standen on the Sussex estate of Wilfrid Scawen Blunt, a cousin of the Wyndhams and an amateur architect. It was typical of Webb that he should choose to spend his last years in an old tile-hung, weather-boarded house of the kind that inspired Standen. Caxtons still stands today and is in reasonable repair, but, sadly, the urban sprawl of 'creepy Crawley' has enveloped it, and only 200 yards away the M23 slices through the once-rural landscape.

The Beales dressed for dinner. When the gong sounded, James and Margaret led the procession from the Drawing Room into the Dining Room, where the blue-green walls were lit by candles, the plates sat warming on the rack over the fireplace, and the table was always decorated with flowers. The Hall was often used for musical evenings, with Amy and her children playing quartets around the Bechstein grand in the bay window alcove. Helen might sing to the party, or Sam do his impersonation of Harry Lauder's 'Roamin' in the Gloamin''. On other evenings there would be games of Pope Joan in the Drawing Room on an old family board, or Racing Demon, Old Maid, Red Nines, Snap and 'Willie's Walk to Grandmama'. Idle young hands

The mace designed by Webb and presented to the newly founded University of Birmingham by Alice Beale in 1902

and minds were always kept busy, sketching, knitting, embroidering, or simply threading beads.

When the family came down to Standen for Christmas, the grandchildren would be herded into the Hall. From the Drawing Room next door would come the noise of rattling fire-irons, as if disturbed by Father Christmas emerging from the chimney. The expectant children would rush in, and there would be the gruff bearded figure, standing by the Christmas tree with their presents.

Maintaining this busy household required a large staff. In the early years there were nine or ten indoor maids, a cook–housekeeper and a butler, with other servants brought down from the Holland Park house for special occasions. Some of the outside staff lodged in a pair of cottages designed by Webb in 1896 with as much care as the main house. They included numerous gardeners and farmworkers, and two coachmen to look after the landau, wagonette and pony trap, which were used for shopping expeditions to East Grinstead or to meet visitors off the train. The Beales fairly early bought

Amy in the Morning Room

Arthur Melville's watercolour of the garden front, painted in 1896 (Business Room)

a car, but maintained their nostalgic allegiance to the horse: a horseshoe was fixed to the car radiator. The elder Beale children became intrepid motorists, and in 1902 Amy is said to have driven all the way to Southampton to meet her younger brother Sydney back from serving in the Boer War. The head coachman, Chapman, was retrained at the Rolls-Royce chauffeur school and promoted to chauffeur when he had learnt to drive. His other job was to wind the clocks in the house every Monday morning.

When James Beale died in 1912, leaving £150,000, the Holland Park house was sold. A large flat was taken on in nearby Campden Hill Court, which became the family's London *pied-à-terre*, and the surplus furniture came down to Standen or was divided among the children's other homes. Standen was vested in a family trust and from then on was run by Margaret Beale and in succession by her two unmarried daughters, Maggie and Helen.

After Roedean, Helen Beale worked as a nurse at the Queen Victoria Hospital in East Grinstead, which had been founded in 1863 as one of the first cottage hospitals. With the outbreak of war in 1914, she found herself looking after Belgian evacuees and convalescent officers who had been sent to Standen. When she came off night duty, she liked to sleep on the roof of the tower, shaded by a canvas awning. She was later posted to France where she worked in a military hospital at Etaples until obliged to return to care for her mother, who was convalescing after an operation. In 1917 she joined the newly formed Women's Royal Naval Service, becoming deputy director of the Chatham Division responsible for the Dover station. Here Wrens acted as drivers and despatch riders, worked on mine netting and gas masks, and heaved sacks of potatoes in the victualling yards. She was awarded the OBE for her work.

Helen's brother Sydney fought in Palestine and Gallipoli, and had to be invalided home with post-diphtherial paralysis and depression. Jack Beale worked in Whitehall managing supplies of wheat to the troops in France; his achievements won him a knighthood. He later became a leading figure in the City, maintaining family connections with the Midlands as chairman of the great Birmingham engineering firm Guest, Keen & Nettlefold (GKN). His younger brother Sam (also later knighted) followed him as chairman, was a director of the London, Midland & Scottish Railway, the successor to the Midland, and a special adviser to the Board of Trade.

The tradition of family gatherings at Standen continued throughout the inter-war years, and a new crop of children began to appear in the nursery corridor, when Amy's offspring married in the mid-1930s. As Margaret Beale got older, she became increasingly deaf. Her temperamental electric hearing aid did not seem to help matters much. As one of her grandchildren put it, 'I always want to consult Granny about things, but it is sometimes difficult to shout my secrets into her ear-trumpet.' By 1932 she could no longer manage the stairs, and so a lift was installed in the entrance courtyard by T. A. Darcy Bradell. (It was removed after the National Trust took over.) She died in 1936 at the age of 89, leaving Maggie and Helen to look after Standen.

The two sisters devoted much of their time to local good works. Maggie founded a home for the mentally ill in Ashdown Forest, known as the Hermitage. In 1936 Helen was appointed vice-chairman of the management board of the newly enlarged Queen Victoria Hospital, and was to remain involved in its running for many years. When the Second World War broke out, the hospital became the centre for the heroic work of Archibald McIndoe, who pioneered plastic surgery for airmen disfigured by burns. During the war years Standen once again took in hospital patients; it was also a sanctuary for those members of the family bombed out of their London homes, and a store-room for their more valued possessions. The garden was turned over almost entirely to growing vegetables, and the house run with the minimum of staff. Helen made one of the more unusual contributions to the war effort by offering her two beloved Irish wolfhounds, Ben and Jinny, as regimental mascots. When Maggie died in 1947, sole responsibility for Standen passed to Helen. She leased the Standen dairy farm from the family company and ran it very successfully with the help of her secretary Nancy Davidson and an excellent bailiff.

In the 1950s and '60s Helen Beale gave important examples of Morris embroidery and metalwork from the house to the Victoria & Albert Museum. She was equally concerned that Standen itself, as one of the few surviving major Webb houses, should be preserved intact after her death. So in November 1971 she approached the National Trust, offering to buy the house and estate from the family trust and bequeath them to the nation. Although the Trust had hitherto accepted only one Victorian country house, Wightwick Manor in Staffordshire (and that principally for its contents), it was persuaded to recognise the architectural importance of Standen. However, the endowment needed to support the property was substantially more than the amount left for the purpose by Helen Beale, when she died in May 1972. Negotiations might have collapsed at this point, if Arthur and Helen Grogan had not stepped in, paying a generous sum for the long lease of the main part of the house and acting as honorary administrators and advisers to the Trust. Much of the present-day success of Standen is due to them for the restoration work they carried out, and for their collecting of furnishings for the house, which had suffered losses of significant contents. The house now attracts over 75,000 visitors a year and has become an essential destination for all those interested in Arts and Crafts architecture and design.

(Opposite) Maggie at her spinning-wheel in the Drawing Room

PLANS OF THE HOUSE

Rooms shown shaded are not open to visitors

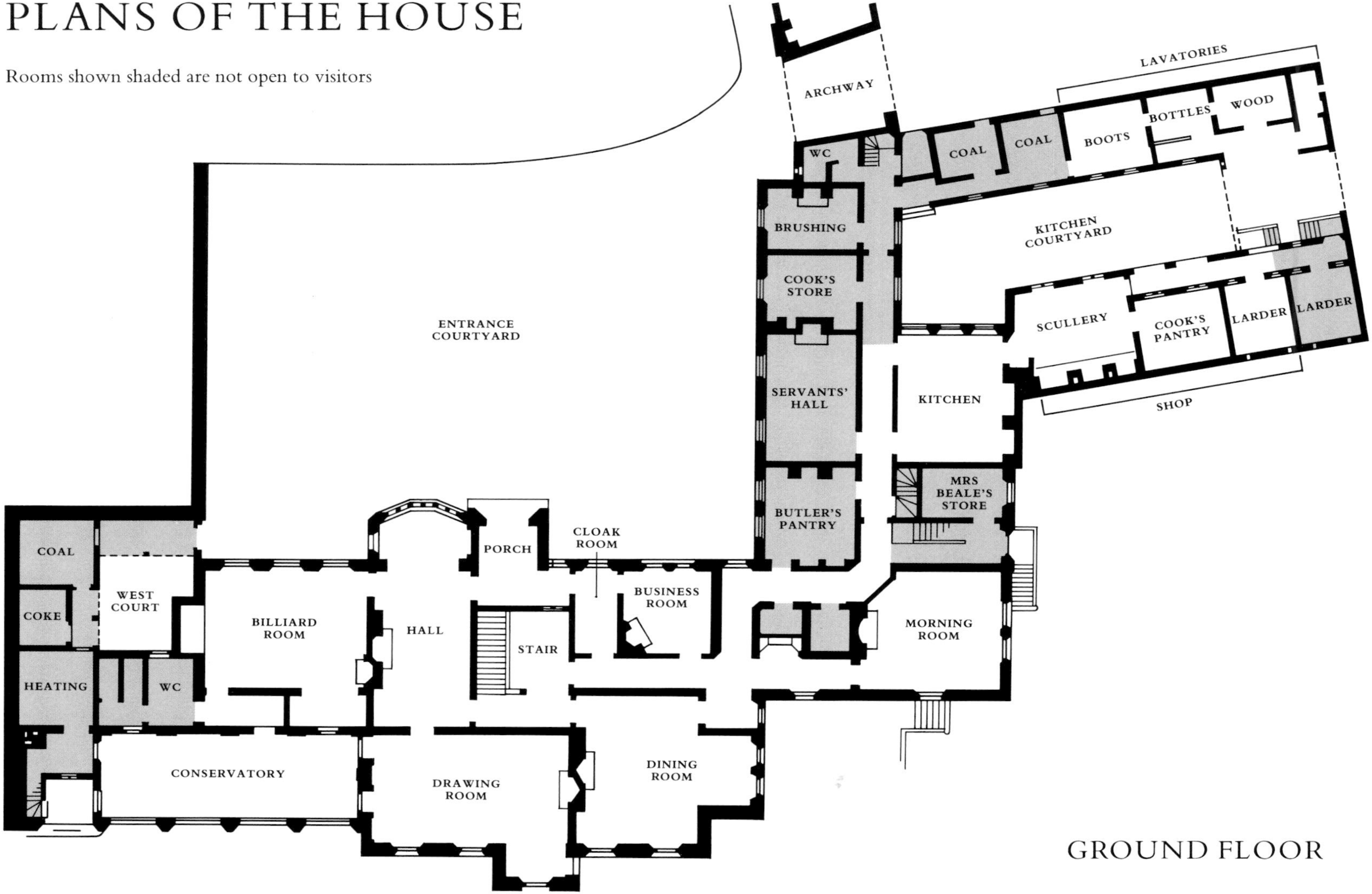

GROUND FLOOR

LAVATORIES

WOOD

BOTTLES

BOOTS

COAL

COAL

ARCHWAY

WC

BRUSHING

COOK'S STORE

SERVANTS' HALL

BUTLER'S PANTRY

KITCHEN COURTYARD

SCULLERY

COOK'S PANTRY

LARDER

LARDER

SHOP

KITCHEN

MRS BEALE'S STORE

MORNING ROOM

BUSINESS ROOM

CLOAK ROOM

DINING ROOM

PORCH

STAIR

HALL

DRAWING ROOM

ENTRANCE COURTYARD

BILLIARD ROOM

CONSERVATORY

WEST COURT

WC

COAL

COKE

HEATING

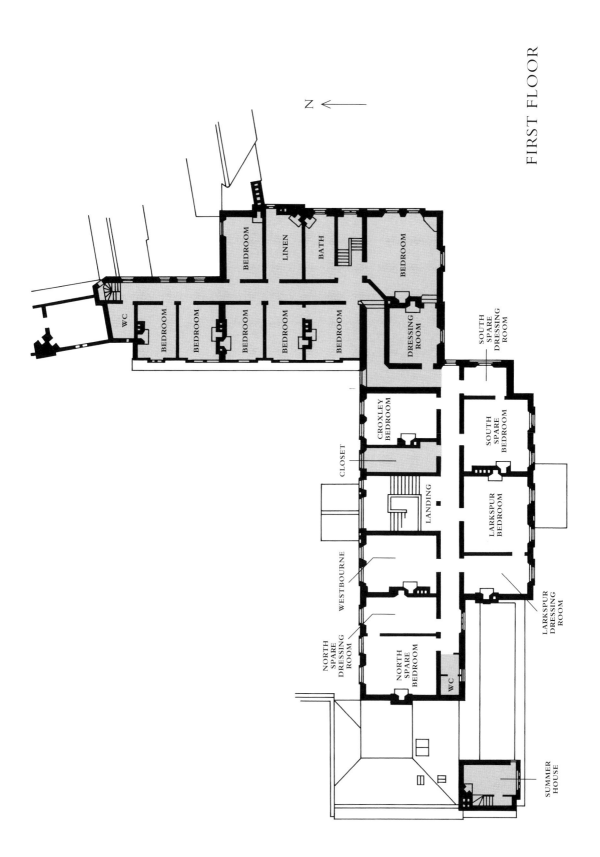

FIRST FLOOR

N ←

BEDROOM
LINEN
BATH
BEDROOM
DRESSING ROOM

WC
BEDROOM
BEDROOM
BEDROOM
BEDROOM
BEDROOM

CLOSET
CROXLEY BEDROOM

SOUTH SPARE DRESSING ROOM

SOUTH SPARE BEDROOM

LANDING

LARKSPUR BEDROOM

WESTBOURNE

LARKSPUR DRESSING ROOM

NORTH SPARE DRESSING ROOM

NORTH SPARE BEDROOM

WC

SUMMER HOUSE

CHAPTER SIX

TOUR OF THE HOUSE

The Exterior

Philip Webb's first set of plans, prepared in May 1891, were reduced in ambition, and, after discussion with the Beales, his revised drawings were completed on 22 August 1891. The position of the house was pegged out in November, with great care taken to save trees near the site. Peter Peters was appointed builder and John Hardy the clerk of works. Building work began in July 1892 and was completed on 25 August 1894, when Webb brought accounts to James Beale. The sequence of work seems to have started with the service wing and Kitchen court, followed by the main block, and, after they were completed, the archway link to Great Hollybush farmhouse. Repairs were made to the farmhouse, and the stable block was the last element to be finished.

THE ENTRANCE COURTYARD

The visitor enters the courtyard of the house using the archway to the right of which is the original Great Hollybush farmhouse (described with the other buildings around Goose Green on p. 73). The materials used for the archway building – horizontal and diamond bands of Horsham stock brick and Keymer rubbed red brick combined with stone quarried on site and local red sand-faced tiles – successfully link the older building materials of the farmhouse with the new house. The leaded windows are also characteristic of some of the service areas of the house.

The east side of the courtyard, which forms part of the kitchen wing, shows Webb's favourite device of a series of weather-boarded gables above a ground floor of brick. The glazing pattern used is the eighteenth-century one of twelve panes in a sash frame, a form revived in the 1870s.

The north elevation is dominated by the water-tower, which is faced with lime-washed roughcast, as Webb felt that brick alone would be inadequate

for a site so exposed to the weather. The tower is crowned by a balustraded viewing platform and a belvedere. The only alteration to have occurred on this elevation was the Hall bay window inserted by Webb in 1898. Stone was used so that it would read as a later addition, in the approved SPAB manner. The neighbouring arch of the Porch is made of receding bands of brick under a wide projecting roof. The combination of two coloured bricks for the façade has a subtlety which is in marked contrast to the harsh polychromy favoured by Webb's mentors, Butterfield and Street.

THE EAST FRONT

This elevation is one of Webb's most complex essays in varied composition. Here the massive, buttress-like chimneystack dominates, but also balances the bulk of the watertower beyond. The recessed planes of the façade combine with tile-hanging to create an ingenious play of shapes and materials. Webb took great care over the structural details of the chimneystacks to guarantee their efficiency and protection from the weather. He specified that the flues were to be lined with 'well made fresh cow-dung mortar not to exceed one-half [inch] thick, laid smoothly and well pressed home with the angles well packed.'

THE SOUTH AND WEST FRONTS

The grouping of five weather-boarded, projecting gables and the window details recall Webb's Joldwynds, near Dorking (1873; demolished) and Coneyhurst, Ewhurst, Surrey (1886). The Conservatory extends the façade at the west end and is terminated by a small belvedere, which balances in miniature the belvedere on top of the watertower. The integration of the five ground-floor bays of the

The entrance courtyard

Conservatory with the rest of the elevation is particularly successful.

The complex roofscape and the varied heights of the different parts of the house indicate Webb's achievement at Standen and are best seen from the top of the quarry and the steps to the Top Terrace.

The Interior

indicates contents original to the house, where not otherwise specified.

THE PORCH

Webb often included a separate porch in his houses to keep down draughts. The exposed wooden beams of the barrel ceiling demonstrate his concern for structural honesty and traditional building materials. The walls are panelled in oak, and the leaded internal window helps to light the inner part of the Staircase Hall.

SCULPTURE

GEORGE FRAMPTON (1860–1928)
The vision, 1893
Bronze relief, with oak frame probably designed by the architect C. F. A. Voysey.

FURNITURE AND WOODWORK

LEFT OF DOOR:

Pokerwork panel of flying birds after a design by Walter Crane, bearing the typically Victorian sentiment 'East or west hame's best'.

Seventeenth-century oak chest, much restored.*

RIGHT OF DOOR:

Light oak bench seat, made by Thomas Henry Kendall of Warwick for Standen in 1894.

THE HALL

The Hall was originally rather shorter; it was lit by two sash windows and Webb's panelling painted dark red. The Beales, who used the room for tea and musical evenings, found it too cramped and gloomy. So in 1898 Webb was asked back to add the bay window and alcove to accommodate the family piano. Unfortunately, the new leaded windows provide little additional light and so the panelling was also repainted white.

During the winter of 2000 the off-white colour chosen by the Beales to replace the initial 'dragon's blood red' scheme has been reinstated. In addition, the two Caucasian runners original to this room have been rewoven giving a closer approximation of the room's appearance at the turn of the century.

CHIMNEY-PIECE

Webb's design seems to be influenced by Vanbrugh and is derived from his drawing-room fireplace for Great Tangley Manor in Surrey in 1885, but with larger side shelves. No two Webb chimney-pieces are identical, at Standen or any of his other houses.

TEXTILES

The stamped velvet window curtains probably came from the Beales' London home, 32 Holland Park, and formerly hung in the Morning Room at Standen. Some of the furniture in the house is also covered in this material.*

FAR RIGHT:

Embroidery hanging, worked by Margaret Beale in 1920–6 with Morris's 'Vine' design for wallpaper of 1873.* The loose structure and naturalism of the pattern is characteristic of Morris's work from 1872 to 1876.

FAR LEFT:

Printed velveteen hanging in Morris's 'Wey' pattern, designed c.1883.

The cushions are covered in Morris's 'Violet and Columbine' woven wool and mohair fabric and 'Crown Imperial' woven cotton.*

The carpets, like most of those in the house, are nineteenth-century Persian and Indian.*

LIGHTING

The hanging electric light-fittings, with opalescent glass shades made by Powell of Whitefriars, were designed by W. A. S. Benson (1854–1924) and installed in 1894. The Benson tubular brass table lamps are also original. (The pleated fabric shades are recent reproductions.) Benson, a protégé of Morris who became managing director of Morris & Co. on his mentor's death in 1896, was an architect and innovator in the design and use of electrical light-fittings. Most of those at Standen are his work.

The Hall

METALWORK

Webb's attention to detail was always fastidious. Note, for instance, the pierced brass fingerplates, which were designed by him.

Silver salver, designed by Omar Ramsden and donated by Dame Jennifer Jenkins.

Circular repoussé metal log-bin, with carrying straps, probably made in Nuremberg around 1900.*

SCULPTURE

FRANCIS WALTER SARGANT (1870–1960)
Margaret Beale (1847–1936)
This marble head of Mrs Beale in old age was sculpted by her nephew in 1931 and exhibited at the RA in 1932.*

PICTURES

School of UKIYO-YE
Seascape with Islands
Woodcut

School of UKIYO-YE
Six Japanese Ladies
Woodcut

School of UKIYO-YE
Three Japanese Prints
Woodcut

FURNITURE

'Manxman' piano
The Beales bought a Bechstein upright for Standen in 1894 and later had a baby concert grand in the Hall. The present model is named after the designer of the prototype, M.H. Baillie Scott (1865–1945), who lived on the Isle of Man. He seems to have taken the idea of enclosing the keyboard with doors from an Elizabethan strongbox. This example was designed by another Arts and Crafts architect, C.R. Ashbee (1863–1942) in 1903, and manufactured by John Broadwood & Sons. The oak cabinet is inlaid with chevron banding and medallions, and decorated with floral enamel plaques. The casework was decorated in imitation of malachite and has now faded to a golden brown.

Walnut x-framed 'Savonarola' chair, probably Italian, mid- or late 19th century.*

Mother-of-pearl and tortoiseshell inlaid chest on stand, the chest made in North Africa during the late 18th century, the mahogany stand supplied by Morris and Company.

The two carved oak, cane chairs were a present to the Beales from Margaret's parents, on loan from the family.

OPPOSITE FIREPLACE:

Side-table, designed by Webb and typical of his plain and sturdy work for Morris & Co.

AROUND ROOM:

Mahogany round occasional table, designed by W.A.S. Benson for Morris & Co.

Mahogany 'Saville' armchair and 'Chippendale' settee, both probably bought from Morris & Co. in 1894 and both upholstered in well-preserved red 'Acorn' stamped velvet.*

Octagonal ivory inlaid 'Damascus' table, bought by the Beales in the Middle East.

Small folding table, by James Shoolbred & Co.*

'Vine' embroidery, which was worked by Margaret Beale in 1920–6 from Morris's wallpaper design of 1873 (Hall)

The Billiard Room

THE BILLIARD ROOM

When first built, the room seems to have been papered with Morris's 'Pomegranate' pattern. The Beales required more room for seating, in addition to the inset settee at the far end of the room, and so in 1898 Webb took in part of the adjoining Conservatory Corridor to create a new alcove, which was papered with 'Pomegranate' to match (still in place). The fireplace across this corner of the room was also moved to its present position. In 1907 George Jack (1855–1932), Webb's chief assistant, introduced the panelling, and also the bookshelves.

LEFT OF FIREPLACE:

Early eighteenth-century English marquetry long-case clock, made by Cornelius Herbert, and much restored.*

CERAMICS

The plum-coloured lustre jug* is from the French factory of Faiencerie du Mont Chevalier, Cannes, and the emerald green dimpled vase with dribble glaze is Burmantofts.

ON MANTELPIECE:

Large majolica pot from the Cantagalli factory in Florence (c.1890), with predominantly blue and yellow floral decoration.*

An Islamic green glass jar and ewer with enamel decoration, bought by Mrs Beale in 1898.

TEXTILES

The window curtains are a reprint of the 'Compton' chintz designed by Morris's senior assistant, J.H. Dearle, for Compton Hall, Warwickshire, c.1896. Morris & Co. also supplied the three brass curtain rods at a cost of £4 3s 5d.*

ON LEATHER SETTEE:

Cushions covered with Morris's 'Tulip and Rose' and 'Musgrove' (centre) patterns.

LIGHTING

OVER BILLIARD TABLE:

Brass-framed light-fitting, probably designed by W. A. S. Benson. The pleated shades of green silk here and elsewhere were renewed by Helen Grogan. The bracket wall lights, the standard and table lamps were also supplied by Benson.

PICTURES

HENRY STACY MARKS, RA (1829–98)
The Seasons
Four chalk drawings.

Photographs of James Beale's youngest daughter, Helen, who bequeathed Standen to the National Trust, of a pencil portrait of her sister, the embroiderer Maggie Beale, and of three of their grandparents.*

FURNITURE

The billiard-table was made by Burroughs & Watts Ltd; the cues, scoreboard and other equipment were supplied by Cox & Yemen of London.*

'Dobbin', the family rocking-horse, was given to the Beales' eldest child Amy in 1874 as a reward for having learnt her alphabet at the age of three. It came down to Standen when the nursery was created on the first floor in 1901 to accommodate the Beales' grandchildren. During the late 1920s when the day nursery was used to accommodate Mrs Beale's nurse, the Beale grandchildren played in the Billiard Room during the day.

IN ALCOVE:

Both cabinets were designed by Ashbee and made by his Guild of Handicraft. The lozenge-shaped panels on the dwarf cabinet to the left have stylised inlaid decoration typical of Ashbee's work. Note also the refined metal sunbursts on the tall cabinet to the right.

Circular tripod 'Arab' table, from Liberty's.*

CERAMICS

ON WALLS AROUND ROOM:

Framed panels of William De Morgan tiles from his Merton Abbey (1882–8) and early Sand's End, Fulham periods (1888–98). The two framed four-tile panels to the right of the leather settee are early experimental designs from De Morgan's Chelsea period (1872–82). For comparison, note the two framed individual tiles on the wall opposite the bookcase, which are not De Morgan, but Iznik – a style which, together with Persian, was a prime influence on De Morgan's ceramic decoration.

ON MANTELPIECE:

Pair of Burmantofts vases in a characteristic turquoise glaze (mid-1880s). Compare these with a large Burmantofts vase of similar colour in the fireplace.

Pair of blue-green Doulton vases (*c*.1920) with a heart-shaped Arts & Crafts leaf pattern.

LEFT OF FIREPLACE:

Elton Ware 'tyg' (or three-handled loving cup).

Vase by Alexander Lauder (*c*.1900), featuring cut-away decoration of birds and tulips in a green glaze.

Clément Massier vase (*c*.1886) in a sea-green and brown streaked glaze.

ON BOOKCASE SHELF:

Elton Ware tankard, dated 1911 in blue slip, made to commemorate George V's coronation.

Ruby and pink lustre decorated De Morgan bowl by Charles Passenger. The interior is decorated with dianthus flowers (a De Morgan favourite) and the exterior with peacocks.

Burmantofts spoon-warmer in the shape of a grotesque toad, again in turquoise glaze.

ABOVE LEATHER SOFA:

Panel of tiles after Benozzo Gozzoli's frescoes of *The Journey of the Magi* in the Palazzo Medici-Riccardi, Florence (1459–61). It was made at the Cantagalli (Chanticleer) works in Florence, as was the lustre charger above, which bears the Medici coat of arms in the centre.

(Opposite) The Conservatory

THE CONSERVATORY CORRIDOR

Before the Billiard Room alcove was built, it connected directly with the Hall.

WALLPAPER

'Trellis', the first wallpaper Morris produced (in 1862), incorporating birds drawn by Webb. It is partly original, but has been much patched and repaired over the years.

TEXTILES

ACROSS END OF CORRIDOR:

Hanging of 'Bird' woven woollen double cloth, designed by Morris in 1878 for the drawing-room at Kelmscott House, Hammersmith.

LIGHTING

Benson hanging ceiling light similar to those in the Hall.

FURNITURE

The glazed cabinet* contains a collection of sea shells replacing that formed by the family.

The Avery scales have always stood in this corridor.

THE CONSERVATORY

The original metal frame supporting the glazed roof was very similar to that Webb designed for the staircase hall in the Middlesbrough offices of Bell Brothers in 1883. It was badly damaged in the 1987 storms and has been replaced. Webb specified unglazed red tiles for the floor as more comfortable to walk on in hob-nailed country boots.

The plants grown here include bougainvillea, oleander and plumbago, which were popular with Edwardian gardeners. Attempts to reintroduce mimosa, a particular favourite of the Beales, have so far been unsuccessful.

LIGHTING

Moorish pierced metal mosque lamp, probably bought from Liberty's.*

THE DRAWING ROOM

This is the first of the three principal ground-floor rooms on the south side of the house, which enjoy the best of the views over the garden and the Medway valley beyond. The alcove at the far end provided a pleasantly private spot for conversation. It has windows only on the south and east sides to ensure that those seated there would not be bothered by direct sunlight in the second half of the day, when the room was most in use.

CHIMNEY-PIECE

The repoussé copper fireplace cheeks, boldly decorated with intertwined sunflowers, were designed by Webb and made by John Pearson (for £8). Webb designed the original fender, which by 1910 had been replaced with the present model, perhaps a Pearson design.

The Liberty's bellows are similarly faced with beaten copper.

The fire-irons were designed by Benson.* In his 1899–1900 catalogue they are priced £2 15s.

WALLPAPER

'Sunflower', designed by Morris in 1879, the decorative motif en suite with the fireplace cheeks and wall sconces. It has been renewed.

TEXTILES

FLANKING CHIMNEY-PIECE:

Hangings of 'Tulip and Rose' woven wool, designed by Morris c.1876. They replace silk embroidery hangings now shown in the North Bedroom.

FLANKING DOORS TO CONSERVATORY:

Curtains of 'Rose' chintz, designed by Morris c.1883.

The damask window curtains are modern, c.1960.*

The hand-knotted wool carpet is a particularly fine example from Merton Abbey, designed by J.H. Dearle, and came to the house through the generosity of the Royal Oak Foundation. Dearle designed all the new carpets made by the firm after 1890.

The embroidered cushions here and elsewhere in the house were worked by members of the family, using both Morris patterns (in this room

The Drawing Room

'Trellis' and 'Pomegranate') and their own original designs.*

METALWORK

Repoussé bronzed copper log-box, by John Pearson, senior metalworker at C. R. Ashbee's Guild of Handicraft, when it started in 1888. Pearson specialised in such decorative repoussé work and brought public attention and popularity to the Guild. The motifs used on the box – ships and birds – evoke the medieval world whose craft guilds were the model for Ashbee's workshop.

LIGHTING

The electric wall lights were designed by Webb especially for this room and made by Pearson. The repoussé copper sconce-plates again feature sunflowers, a favourite motif of the contemporary Aesthetic movement. Webb allowed Pearson some freedom in interpreting his design, as no two are identical. Powell of Whitefriars supplied the glass twists that decorate the flex and the opalescent fluted shades.

The standard and table lamps were designed by W. A. S. Benson.

PICTURES

John Buxton Knight (1843–1908)
A river estuary

Dame Ethel Walker (1861–1951)
Tea in the garden

James Aumonier (1832–1911)
Misty sunrise

James Charles (1851–1906)
Haymaking

James Charles (1851–1906)
Scything

Maggie Beale (1872–1947)
A Japanese scene
Watercolour.*

John Buxton Knight (1843–1908)
Wemys agrimony

James Aumonier (1832–1911)
Misty landscape

James Charles (1851–1906)
Bosham Mill

Edward Stott (1859–1918)
Red Roses

SCULPTURE

Albert Toft (1862–1949)
Mother and child, 1899
Bronze.

FURNITURE

AROUND ROOM:

The easy chairs, which include the 'Connaught' model, were supplied mostly by Morris & Co, and upholstered in green Morris stamped mohair or 'Utrecht Velvet', now very faded.*

'Old English or Jacobean' armchair, designed by E. W. Godwin (1833–86) for the furniture-maker William Watt about 1877, and much copied.

Rosewood armchair upholstered in green velvet, by Collinson & Lock.

Morris & Co. pie-crust edge, six-legged occasional table, designed by George Jack. The stretcher, coincidently, features a sunflower.

A decagonal Moorish coffee table, inlaid with mother-of-pearl.

AGAINST LEFT WALL:

Glazed and inlaid china cabinet, also designed by Jack and described in the Morris catalogue as 'of highest Sheraton finish'.

Settee, probably designed by Agnes and Rhoda Garrett, and upholstered in very faded red 'Utrecht Velvet'. The tapering, square-section legs are typical of their furniture, and can be seen in the upholstered footstools also in this room.*

IN ALCOVE:

Morris 'Chippendale' mahogany double settee, also upholstered in 'Utrecht Velvet'. Furniture designed by the firm from the 1880s often recalls eighteenth-century patterns, either in modified versions, or, as here, in more or less faithful reproductions.*

AGAINST WINDOW WALL:

Elaborately inlaid rosewood cabinet, designed by Stephen Webb, and made by Collinson & Lock. The marquetry decoration is intended to suggest sixteenth-century grotesque ornament. The high quality of the firm's workmanship made it expensive and sought after.

George III clock, signed 'James Leumas'.*

The other furniture is either antique or reproduction. The combination of contemporary and eighteenth-century pieces would have appealed to Webb.

CERAMICS

IN SMALL GLAZED CABINET:

Some fine examples of William De Morgan's pottery, mostly ruby lustre vases from his early Sand's End, Fulham period (1888–98). The tazza (or shallow bowl on stand) was designed by Charles Passenger, and the tile featuring a galleon in full sail is a splendid example of De Morgan's use of multi-coloured enamels. The cabinet also contains a late Ruskin porcelain bowl (1924) and a Martin Brothers gourd-shaped vase (1909).

ON TOP OF CABINET:

William De Morgan bowl in his 'Persian Colours', decorated by Jim Hersey. The bowl was a 25th wedding anniversary present to James and Margaret Beale from their children in April 1895.*

IN OTHER CABINETS:

Chinese porcelain, with a Japanese part tea-service near the window.

ON TOP OF LEFT WALL CABINET:

Pair of Doulton drug jars by Mark V. Marshall, and a blue and mauve double vase by William Baron.

AT FRONT OF ROOM:

Late Fulham ruby lustre bowl by De Morgan, decorated by his premier assistant, Fred Passenger.

IN FIREPLACE:

Large Brannam vase by Charles Brannam himself; there are other Brannam pieces around the room.

ABOVE FIREPLACE:

Italian charger featuring blue and green Iznik decoration, and dated 1881.

ON THE INLAID TABLE:

Elton cache-pot (ornamental flowerpot).

THE STAIRCASE AND INNER HALL

Webb's flat banisters are a revival of 17th-century 'flat' balustrades. The deep shelves on the half-landing and first-floor landing allowed plenty of room for displaying china.

A good representation of William De Morgan's ruby lustre decorated pottery from his experimental period (c.1880) to his early Sand's End, Fulham period (1888–98). The pieces exhibit a range of decorative subjects and styles, from winged mythical beasts, fish and lizards to Persian floreate patterns and cherubic figures of the Italian Renaissance. These ceramics are displayed in a satinwood cabinet in the style of the Misses Garrett.

WALLPAPER

'Bachelor's Button', designed by Morris in 1892. It was varnished to protect it from scuffing, and repaired in 1906; it continues into the Bedroom Corridor.

TEXTILES

The original Patent Axminster stair-carpet and rugs were supplied by the Morris firm in 1906 together with the present curtains and wallpaper.

Only part of the original carpet survives in store and is a fragile and rare example of the chenille weaving techniques that used both machine and hand weaving. Through the generous donations of visitors and benefactors of Standen it has been possible to copy and restore the carpet to its original arrangement during the winter of 2000.

PICTURES

FORD MADOX BROWN (1821–93)
The Baptism of King Edwin
Twelve wall-paintings illustrating the history of Manchester were commissioned in 1878 from Ford Madox Brown to decorate Alfred Waterhouse's recently completed Manchester Town Hall. This is a full-size replica of the preliminary cartoon (now in the National Gallery of Victoria, Melbourne) for the second scene in the series, which was the first to be painted (between July 1878 and July 1880). It illustrates the key event in the Saxon history of Manchester, the introduction of Christianity to the city. The finished cycle was Madox Brown's most ambitious achievement and ranks among the greatest of Victorian murals, but the scale of the task destroyed his health.

WILLIAM NICHOLSON (1872–1949)
James Beale (1840–1912)
A successful London solicitor who commissioned Webb to build Standen in 1891. Painted, like the portrait of his wife in the Hall, in 1905.*

The Staircase Hall

WILLIAM NICHOLSON (1872–1949)
Margaret Beale (1847–1936)
The decoration of Standen and the character of the
garden reflect the taste of this cultivated and
energetic woman, who married James Beale in
1870. Painted in 1905.*

KENNETH GREEN (1938)
Sir Samuel Beale

SCULPTURE

ON HALF-LANDING:

ALFRED DRURY (1856–1944)
The Age of Innocence
Drury exhibited a version at the RA in 1897. Several
bronze casts are known, and it was later reworked in
marble.

GEORGE FRAMPTON (1860–1928)
Mary and Agnes
Framed plaster relief.

CERAMICS

ON HALF-LANDING:

Two large vases by Clément Massier: one, a large turquoise, streaked glaze vase with cylindrical neck; the other a contrasting celadon glaze with carved lions.*

Pair of Pilkington vases in a mottled turquoise glaze (1903–4).

THE BEDROOM CORRIDOR

Of the twelve bedrooms on the first floor, which were used by James and Margaret Beale, their elder children and guests, four were given dressing-rooms, but Webb included only one bathroom and two lavatories, expecting the Beales to rely on washstands, hip-baths and commodes with carried water and slops. Most of this floor is now privately occupied and at present three bedrooms and two dressing-rooms are shown.

TEXTILES

St Agnes tapestry
The figure is based on a design produced by Burne-Jones for stained glass; the foliage background was added by Morris. This design was first woven in 1887, with a matching *St Cecilia*, for Sir Thomas Wardle, the Staffordshire fabric dyer and printer who had produced most of Morris's early textiles.

METALWORK

Repoussé copper charger by Pearson.

PICTURES

Most of the pictures hanging in the Bedroom Corridor are prints after masterpieces by Italian Renaissance artists. An important exception is the reproduction of Burne-Jones's *The Golden Stairs* (Tate Gallery).*

FURNITURE

Rush-seated 'Sussex' ebonised chairs, four designed by Ford Madox Brown for Morris & Co. and one by Webb to traditional patterns.

Late seventeenth-century chest, veneered with laburnum, on a later stand.*

Liberty's oak bookcase.

CERAMICS

Brannam tankard plus a pair of Doulton vases and urn (c.1895) in a mottled blue and brown glaze.

Early Brannam harvest jug, featuring stylised Passion flowers on a chocolate brown ground (1880).

A pair of Burmantofts vases with loop handles, each featuring a bird with a snake in its claws (c.1895).

THE LARKSPUR BEDROOM

This and the adjoining dressing-room were originally fitted up for the Beales' eldest daughter, Amy. The built-in wardrobes, with the fitted mirror in the door, were designed by Webb for her.

WALLPAPER

'Larkspur', designed by Morris in 1874, and last renewed in 1937.

TEXTILES

The curtains are modern reprints of the 'Scroll' pattern, adapted c.1895 from the background of Morris's 'Powdered' wallpaper, which can be seen in the North Bedroom.

Late nineteenth-century English velvet-pile carpet with a Morris-inspired pattern.

FURNITURE

The matching mahogany chest of drawers, dressing-table, linen press and bedside table are superb examples of the cabinetmaking skills of Ernest Gimson (1864–1919), the Arts and Crafts designer who set up his workshop in the Cotswolds in 1895. They all have their original silver handles and were recently acquired for Standen with the generous support of the MGC/V&A Purchase Grant Fund.

The brass bed, like the others in the house, was bought from Heal's in 1894.

Rush-seated lyre-backed armchair, designed by D. G. Rossetti for Morris & Co.

Day-bed upholstered in its original gold stamped mohair, by Agnes and Rhoda Garrett. The bed is illustrated in the Garretts' *Suggestions for Home Decoration in Painting, Woodwork and Furniture* (1876).*

CERAMICS

ON MANTELPIECE:

Pair of blue Doulton vases decorated with a floral pattern and pieces by Della Robbia and Elton.

A pink flower vase by Pilkington.

A pair of flower patterned vases by Barum.

THE LARKSPUR DRESSING ROOM

The stained green floorboards are original.

WALLPAPER

This room has been papered with 'Larkspur' since at least 1906. It was originally hung with a textile.

TEXTILES

Like those in the Larkspur Bedroom, the window curtains are a modern reprint of 'Scroll'.

METALWORK

OVER THE WASHSTAND:

Austrian 'Secessionist' mirror with brass frame, c.1900.

ON FIREPLACE TRIVET:

Brass and copper kettle, designed by Christopher Dresser (1834–1904).

PICTURE

JAMES FRAYER
Girl in a blue dress

FURNITURE

A Morris 'Chippendale' mahogany chair upholstered in green stamped velvet.*

'Old English or Jacobean' ebonised armchair. Perhaps made by Collier & Plunkett in the late nineteenth century after the original design by E. W. Godwin, and similar to that in the Drawing Room.*

The linen press is in the style of Voysey.

Occasional table, also after a design by E. W. Godwin of 1867. There is a similar table in the Morning Room.

The rosewood washstand was part of a five-piece suite supplied by Collinson & Lock in 1896.*

CERAMICS

Cauldon Ware jug and basin set by Brown-Westhead, Moore & Co., dated 1886–8.*

GLASS

Green glass vases by Powell of Whitefriars on metal stands.*

THE WESTBOURNE BEDROOM

This room was used for many years by Maggie Beale as her embroidery studio.

WALLPAPER

'Willow Bough', designed by Morris in 1887 and renewed in the mid-1970s.

TEXTILES

The curtains are 'Tulip' printed cotton, designed by Morris c.1875. They are believed to have come to Standen in the 1950s from the London home of the Beales' son Samuel.

LIGHTING

The table lamps were designed by Benson to stand on bedside tables or hang from the wall. He was the first to produce this kind of 'metamorphic' fitting, which was much imitated.*

PICTURES

EDWIN ELLIS (1841–95)
A moorland scene
Watercolour.

ROBERT WEIR ALLAN (1852–1942)
A Scottish glen
Watercolour.

ROBERT ANNING BELL, RA (1863–1933)
Charity
Coloured plaster relief.

FURNITURE

The inlaid satinwood wardrobe and dressing-table with adjustable oval mirror may have been designed by the Garretts in the 1870s.*

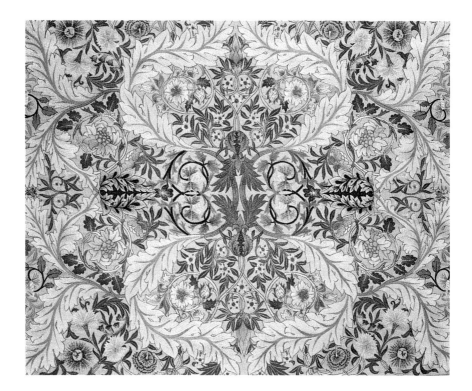

Part of the 'Acanthus' pattern embroidery, worked with silk and worsted wool, c.1896

The mahogany and satinwood washstand with a Brescia marble top is Edwardian, in the Sheraton style.

Collection of Burmantofts vases in a turquoise glaze.

Jug and basin set in the Minton 'Cockatrice' pattern, and a Minton white china slop bucket.*

THE NORTH SPARE BEDROOM

WALLPAPER

'Powdered', designed by Morris in 1874, hung in 1985.

TEXTILES

Embroidered hangings
These were embroidered in silk about 1896 by Margaret Beale and her three eldest daughters, and at one time hung flanking the Drawing Room fireplace. They are based on Morris's 'Artichoke' design, which had originally been commissioned by Ada Godman for hangings to decorate the drawing-room of Smeaton Manor in Yorkshire, the country house Webb built for the Godmans in 1876–7. The version embroidered by Ada Godman over many years was in wool on a linen backing, and is now divided between the Victoria & Albert Museum, the William Morris Art Gallery, Walthamstow, and the Fitzwilliam Museum, Cambridge.

The curtains are a modern reprint of the 'Lodden' chintz, designed by Morris in 1884.

The carpet is a Kidderminster, woven with Morris's 'Tulip and Lily' pattern of c.1875 by the Heckmondwike Company.

The cushion is covered with 'Squirrel' woven woollen fabric, designed by J. H. Dearle c.1898.

The Acanthus patterned embroidery executed with silk and woollen yarns c.1896 in the Morris & Co. workshops under the direction of May Morris.

Panel of silk embroidery, originally for a firescreen, was given to Standen in 1986. The embroidered poppies, on a linen ground, is original to the house.*

PICTURES

EDWARD BURNE-JONES (1833–98)
Seated Girl

THOMAS MATTHEWS ROOKE (1842–1942)
Venice
Watercolour

FURNITURE

The elaborately inlaid rosewood wardrobe and bedside cabinet are part of a suite made for Standen by Collinson & Lock in 1896 at a cost of £294.

Mahogany writing-table, mid-Georgian.

A Heal's brass bedstead.*

THE NORTH SPARE DRESSING ROOM

WALLPAPER

'Powdered', designed by Morris in 1874.

TEXTILES

The curtains are a modern reprint of the 'Lodden' chintz, designed by Morris in 1884.

FURNITURE

Elaborately inlaid rosewood dressing-table and washstand, designed for Standen by Collinson & Lock.

PICTURES

FREDERICK SANDYS (1829–1904)
Selene
Coloured chalks.
Sandys began his career as a follower of the Pre-Raphaelites, but after about 1869 he gave up painting in oils almost entirely to concentrate on elaborate chalk drawings of beautiful women with expressive chins, such as this.

Attributed to BURNE-JONES (1833–98)
A women's head
Chalk.

GEORGE HOWARD, 9th EARL OF CARLISLE (1843–1911)
Portrait of a woman
Coloured chalks.
As a young man Howard commissioned Philip

The Collinson & Lock washstand in the North Dressing Room

Webb to build 1 Palace Green, Kensington, which became a showplace for Pre-Raphaelite art and Morris decoration.

HENRY HOLIDAY (1839–1927)
Two drawings of angels and saints
Under the influence of the Pre-Raphaelites, Holiday designed much work for stained glass, which was made by Powell of Whitefriars and, after 1890, at his own glassworks.

WILLIAM BLAKE RICHMOND, RA (1842–1921)
Prometheus
Pair of drawings of female nudes

DANTE GABRIEL ROSSETTI (1828–82)
A woman's head
Coloured chalks, dated 1867.

Studio of BURNE-JONES
St Matthew
Chalk.

CERAMICS

Copeland jug and basin set in the 'Indian Tree' pattern (1886)*; a Della Robbia plate by Charles Collis; and some pieces by Brannam, including a spill vase with peacock design by James Dewdney (1887).

THE DINING ROOM

The green painted panelling, although repainted at least once, follows the original scheme. It is combined with blue-and-white Chinese porcelain in a manner first revived by Rossetti and much favoured by Morris and Webb.

FIREPLACE

Webb designed the entire ensemble: the trelliswork and the pierced central and side panels of the fender echo the forms of the overmantel and fretwork panel above. The repoussé mild steel cheeks and smoke cowel were based on a design he had produced for the picture gallery fireplace of Constantine Ionides's house in Hove in 1890–1, and were made by John Pearson. The grate, plate rack and fender were made by Thomas Elsley, a London blacksmith often employed by Webb. The coal scuttle came from Benham & Sons in 1894.

TEXTILES

The curtains are 'Peacock and Dragon' woven woollen cloth, designed by Morris in 1878. They were ordered for Standen in 1897 at a cost of £35 8s.

Two Feraghan carpets, cut to fit and now very worn.

METALWORK

The silverplated copper hot-plate with two covered dishes, the pair of brass and copper candlesticks, the table lamp with cream shade, and most of the metalwork in the room are by Benson.

Silverplated muffin-dish, designed by C. R. Ashbee c.1900.

Silver cake basket, given to James and Margaret Beale on their marriage in 1870.

PICTURES

JAMES CHARLES (1851–1906)
Girl in white

STANHOPE FORBES, RA (1857–1947)
Ferryman at Flushing

HENRY HERBERT LA THANGUE (1859–1929)
Portrait of a boy

The Dining Room fireplace

Forbes and La Thangue were friends and leading members of the Newlyn School, active in this Cornish fishing village at the turn of the century.

HENRY HERBERT LA THANGUE (1859–1929)
Portrait of a woman

STANHOPE FORBES, RA (1857–1947)
Children in the street

JOHN BUXTON KNIGHT (1843–1908)
A River Estuary

FURNITURE

The two fitted dressers were designed by Webb, but his intended serving-table was not carried out and

Dorothy Beale trying on a dress in the Dining Room

the present sideboard may be by Llewellyn Rathbone, who certainly made its drop handles. The form of the dressers, with raised platforms underneath the drawers, recalls Webb's dining-room at Rounton Grange in Yorkshire (1872–6) for Sir Lowthian Bell.

The dining-table and chairs, based on eighteenth-century models and made from Spanish mahogany, were supplied by S. & H. Jewell & Co. in 1894. The seats were embroidered in wool by Maggie Beale and other members of the family with their own designs and others supplied by the Royal School of Art Needlework.

BETWEEN DRESSERS:

Early eighteenth-century circular red walnut table.*

BETWEEN WINDOWS:

Oak cabinet, possibly made by Morris & Co. in the late nineteenth century.*

CERAMICS

The finest piece is a mid-sixteenth-century Chinese ewer decorated with a magic fountain design. This design has been related to a 'Magic Fountain' reputed to have been built by the Paris goldsmith Guillaume Bouchier for Mangu Khan at Karakoram in 1254, but it may equally be based on a contemporary Italian Renaissance fountain. Nine similar ewers are in the Topkapi Serai Museum, Istanbul, one of which is virtually identical, with a similar mark: *yong bao chang chun (Forever [or eternal] preserve [or protection] enduring [or ?late] spring)*.

GLASS

Claret jug with silverplated mounts, by Christopher Dresser.

Cut-glass bowls and covered vases, *c*.1830–50.

THE MORNING ROOM CORRIDOR

The slate shelf in the lobby outside the Dining Room was designed by Webb to take trays of food on their way from the Kitchen to table; the radiator beneath helped to keep them warm. Webb also designed the recessed dresser with flanking cupboards and a characteristically coved ceiling above.

The chamfered corners and simple plaster details should also be noted.

WALLPAPER

Like the Conservatory Corridor, this is hung with the 'Trellis' wallpaper, much repaired and renewed, but in considerable part original.

METALWORK

LEFT OF DINING ROOM DOOR:

Convex mirror, with repoussé copper frame by C. R. Ashbee and Pearson.

PICTURES

EDWARD STOTT (1858–1918)
Watering Place

TERRICK WILLIAMS, RA (1860–1908)
*The restless sea**

Sir ERNEST WATERLOW, RA (1850–1919)
Rocky coast

THOMAS MATTHEWS ROOKE (1842–1942)
Malmesbury Abbey
Notre Dame de Semur
Rocques, near Lisieux
Canterbury Cathedral
Cremona
Watercolours
In the 1880s Rooke was one of several artists engaged by Ruskin on behalf of the SPAB to record European cathedrals and other historic buildings threatened by decay and crude restoration. He was also for many years studio assistant to Burne-Jones.

FURNITURE

Mahogany bookcase, probably designed by the Garretts.*

CERAMICS

ON SERVING SLAB:

Large Della Robbia pot by Gertrude Russell and Charles Collis, c.1903.*

ON DRESSER:

English and continental Delft pottery.*

THE MORNING ROOM

Facing east, this room gets the best of the morning light. It was used mostly by the women of the house.

TEXTILES

The original wall-hangings of 'Daffodil' chintz, designed by Dearle c.1891, have been recreated, although the colour is not completely accurate. A fragment of the original, now somewhat faded, material has been used to cover one of the cushions on the settee.*

Other cushions are covered in Morris 'Crown Imperial' and 'Tulip' fabric.*

LIGHTING

The light-fittings are original and the lamps are by Benson.

METALWORK

Pair of brass candlesticks, by Benson.

Repoussé brass fender and copper jardinière, by Pearson, and two-handled tankard is by John Williams.

SCULPTURE

FRANCIS DERWENT WOOD (1871–1926)
Anne Dinnage
Marble.
Housekeeper to Wood's friend, the painter Edward Stott.

FURNITURE

The mahogany corner-cupboard, the pair of low armchairs with ball finials and characteristic tapering legs, and the footstool were designed by the Garretts and bought by the Beales for their London house in the 1870s. They are all illustrated in the Garretts' *Suggestions for Home Decoration*.

IN CENTRE OF ROOM:

Oval mahogany seven-legged table, designed by Webb for Morris & Co.*

The tub armchair and settee have loose covers of the 'Golden Lily' pattern designed by Dearle for wallpaper, and not sold by Morris & Co. as a fabric.*

The 'Morris' adjustable chair is based on a traditional Sussex type, and upholstered in Morris
'Snakeshead' chintz.

The Morris 'Sunbury' armchair is upholstered in
'Windrush' chintz.

Small, six-legged occasional table, designed by
George Jack for Morris & Co.

Liberty's three-legged Wyllie tea-cup stand.

*(Top) Della Robbia majolica charger; by Harold
Rathbone, 1896. (Bottom) Willow pattern plate; by
Thackeray Turner, 1885 (Morning Room)*

The glazed bureau-cabinet containing the family's
Rockingham tea-service is by T. E. Collcutt and
may have been made by Collinson & Lock; it
probably once had an upper stage.

Mantel clock with blue-and-white enamel panels,
made by J. W. Benson of Bond Street, and probably
designed by Lewis F. Day, an influential late nineteenth-century writer on design.

CERAMICS

Collection of Della Robbia vases and chargers, most
notable of which is the charger with the head of
Sylvia (captioned 'Who is Sylvia?'), dated 1896, by
Harold Rathbone, the founder of the pottery.

Plate by Carlo Manzoni in Italianate style, also
dated 1896.

Other pieces include vases by Elton, Brannam,
Doulton and the French potter Léon Castel; and
two plates by Thackeray Turner (a willow pattern
and floral pattern, dated 1885 and 1883 respectively)
above the fireplace. Turner was an architect and
disciple of Webb, and decorated pottery.

ABOVE BOOKCASE:

Large planter with loop handles and deep blue
glaze, by Christopher Dresser.

ON TABLE:

Blue lustre charger from De Morgan's late Fulham
period (1898–1907), with decoration of two lion-
esses by Charles Passenger.

GLASS

The green glass vases are probably by Powell of
Whitefriars.*

THE BUSINESS ROOM

This was used by James Beale as his study. The
joinery was originally painted red; the wall to
the right of the windows also once had a window
(now blocked) placed high to light the Kitchen
Corridor.

WALLPAPER

Like the wallpaper in the North Bedroom, the
'Poppy' paper here has been reprinted using the
original Morris & Co. blocks.

TEXTILES

The curtains are 'Bird and Vine' woven woollen fabric, designed by Morris c.1879. They were ordered in 1894.*

LIGHTING

The hanging glass shade is not a Benson design, but has always been in this position.

METALWORK

Pearson repoussé copper fender.

PICTURES

HERBERT MARSHALL (1841–1913)
St Margaret's, Westminster, 1887
The view from the windows of Beale & Co.'s London offices.*

ARTHUR MELVILLE (1855–1904)
The garden front of Standen
Signed and dated 1896.

FURNITURE

Liberty's oak cabinet, with doors carved with linen-fold decoration.

Walnut tallboy, made by the Cotswolds cabinet-maker Edward Barnsley in 1936. (On loan, like the following two pieces, from the Holburne of Menstrie Museum, Bath.)

Walnut writing-desk, made by Henry Davoll in 1921.

Walnut cabinet, made by Eric Sharpe in 1943.

CERAMICS

ON DESK:

Doulton stoneware jug decorated in brown by Frank Butler, and a pair of Doulton vases.

THE CLOAK ROOM

FURNITURE

Light oak bench seat, copied from the old 'Saxon' chair in Lord Leycester's Hospital in Warwick, made by Thomas Henry Kendall of Warwick in 1894 for Standen.

THE EAST CORRIDOR

The floor is paved with York stone and unglazed red tiles.

THE KITCHEN

The kitchen was redecorated 2001–2 to a scheme introduced originally by the Beale family, and kept until the 1960s.

The cast-iron range was supplied by Smith & Wellstood Ltd, of Ludgate Circus, London, and was never changed. The kitchen table from Maple's is also original. Webb designed the dressers and fitted cupboards in the servants' quarters.

METALWORK

Among the copper dishes is a muffin dish by W. A. S. Benson.

The cast-iron Kitchen range, which was supplied by Smith & Wellstood Ltd

CHAPTER SEVEN
THE GARDEN

Standen takes its name from one of the three farms, Great Hollybush, Stone and Standen, which James Beale purchased in 1890. Standen farmhouse was a small low-pitched cottage which stood to the south of the present house, and was demolished in 1896. It was Great Hollybush farmhouse which Philip Webb incorporated into the new house. The first reference to this farm is in 1587 (in the *Buckhurst Terrier*) and the earliest map of the estate is dated 1776. Some of the names given to the fields in documents as early as 1615 were still in use in 1970, when Helen Beale purchased the estate from the family trustees. A great advantage the garden possesses is the view to the south-east over Weir-wood reservoir to Ashdown Forest and Crowborough Beacon. Sharpthorne and West Hoathly are to the south-west.

The Beales started planting the garden almost immediately after they had acquired the land. In the spring of 1891 trees were planted, a yew hedge established and the kitchen garden begun. They consulted a London landscape gardener, G. B. Simpson, who drew up a planting layout that anticipated a site for the new house on the line of the existing terrace. As described in Chapter Three, Webb suggested to the Beales that the house be re-sited further into the hillside. On Simpson's earlier work for the garden he superimposed immediately to the south of his new house the terrace walk, which was bordered by a simple wooden trellis similar to that at the Red House.

Simpson's planting schemes were in the so-called 'gardenesque' manner, with strict geometrical layouts of colourful flowerbeds and shrubs. Webb's preferences were quite different. The architect had taken great care with the design of the garden at Clouds where he had mixed natural styles of planting with some 'old-fashioned' formality and compartment gardens. William Robinson (1838–1935), a neighbour of the Beales at Gravetye Manor, was the most influential late nineteenth-century advocate of the natural approach to planting, using wild and simple flowers. A vociferous critic of the formal artificiality of High Victorian gardens, he admired Webb's work at Clouds, which he described thus: 'As regards the best new houses, Clouds, so well built by Mr Philip Webb, is not any the worse for its picturesque surroundings which do not meet the [usual] architect's senseless craving for order and balance.' Another important garden by Webb was at Great Tangley Manor, near Guildford in Surrey (1885), where he skilfully combined traditional materials and a compartment layout, which was planted with old varieties of flowers and shrubs.

The characteristic Arts and Crafts garden used local materials in the construction of the formal elements, and loose planting within an unpretentious framework of yew hedges, trellis and pergolas. Naturalistic colour schemes and unforced combinations of colour and foliage were preferred, and care was also taken in the transition between the garden and the surrounding landscape. The garden at Standen contains many of these typical features, but Simpson's influence and Margaret Beale's interests as a plantswoman gave it a less subdued and occasionally more exotic character than Webb would have preferred. Yet although the garden was never a doctrinaire essay in Arts and Crafts theory, its overall structure and harmony with the landscape make it as typical of the period as the house itself.

Margaret Beale's garden diary allows us accurately to reconstruct the development of the garden and her constant revisions to the planting. The drive was made through an old quarry with

(Opposite) The east front from the Rose Garden

The Top Terrace and summer-house

dramatic effect and a new quarry was opened, west of the Conservatory, to provide building stone for the house. The south, garden terrace was begun in October 1893, the rock garden was planted with heather and conifers from October 1896 and completed in February 1897. In 1910 the firm of J. Cheal & Sons created the Top Terrace and summer-house in a similar style to Webb's earlier work in the garden. This terrace was aligned exactly with West Hoathly church, which can be seen beyond the summer-house. A rose garden later to become the bamboo garden was created for bathing, and a court for tennis on the lawn below and to the south-east

of the house (now known as the Croquet Lawn). With Mrs Beale's diary, there survive her plant catalogues of alpines, Japanese trees and shrubs, and other exotics, many of which can still be seen in the garden.

After Margaret Beale's death in 1936 the period of experimentation ended and her daughters did little to change their mother's plantings. Some consolidation of overmature shrubberies has been inevitable since the Trust took responsibility for the garden, and the garden and woodlands have taken time to recover from the effects of the storms of the 1980s and 1990s. Nevertheless, it remains a garden with much to interest the historian and plantsman alike.

GOOSE GREEN

The Green is bounded to the west by the tile-hung Hollybush Farm, which dates from around 1450, to the north by the seventeenth-century weather-boarded barn, restored and extended by a protégé of Webb (now the Tea-room and Information Room), and to the south by the service wing of Webb's new house. On Webb's original plans it is described simply as the 'House Green'. It takes its present name from the geese that were raised here for the Standen table. Geese had the additional advantage of being excellent guard-dogs.

On the Green are three London Planes and a Medlar.

THE COURTYARD

Around the gravelled Courtyard to the north of the house *Bergenia crassifolia* and *B. cordifolia* grow at the foot of the walls.

An alternative steep route may be taken round the garden starting from the steps on the north side of the Courtyard, passing the top of the Quarry Garden to join the Top Walk. There are some dramatic views here across the garden to the countryside beyond.

THE MULBERRY LAWN

In the centre of the lawn is a young Black Mulberry (*Morus nigra*) and nearby an English Yew, one of the few trees in the garden which is older than the house. Webb marked it carefully on his first plans for Standen and ensured that it was preserved. On the walls of the house here are the Banksian Rose, *Rosa banksiae* 'Lutea', wisteria and clematis.

THE TERRACE

The east end of the terrace contains Fuchsia, camellias and lilies, overhung with acers and the late-flowering Chaste-Tree (*Vitex agnus-castus*), cultivated in Britain since 1520. At the other end of the Terrace *Ceanothus impressus* 'Puget Blue' is a fine sight in late spring. Also growing on the wall here is

the Chilean *Azara microphylla*, with vanilla-scented yellow flowers in spring.

Plants in the south-facing border include lavender, *Agapanthus*, *Crinodendron hookerianum* and *Yucca gloriosa*, with wall shrubs and climbers such as *Buddleja alternifolia* and *Clematis armandii*.

THE QUARRY GARDEN

The quarry, which provided the stone for the house, holds a collection of Mollis azaleas, *Rhododendron luteum* with its fragrant rich yellow flowers in May, and the self-clinging *Hydrangea petiolaris*. The Royal Ferns (*Osmunda regalis*) are probably descended from the original dozen plants supplied by Messrs Waterer in 1891. Many cristate (crested) forms of ferns also grow here, with primulas and anemones.

Either side of the steps to the Top Walk are Japanese Maples (*Acer japonicum* and *A. palmatum*), *Magnolia × soulangeana* and camellias including *C. japonica* 'Nobilissima', *C. × williamsii* 'Donation' and *C. saluenensis* 'Bow Bells'. Below some of the shrubs can be found the curious Mouse-tail Plant (*Arisarum proboscideum*). Epimedium also thrive in this area.

THE TOP TERRACE

Between the Quarry Garden and the Top Terrace, the path passes more Japanese Maples including *Acer palmatum* 'Heptalobum Elegans Purpureum' and brightly coloured Ghent azaleas.

The Top Terrace was designed by J. Cheal & Sons and dates from 1910. It is flanked to the north by yellow *Azalea pontica*, with views across Weirwood reservoir and Ashdown Forest south-east toward Crowborough Beacon. The path from the south-west end of the Terrace continues to the left giving views of the surrounding countryside and to the right along a recently replanted woodland walk leading back to the house.

THE UPPER LAWN

The centre of the lawn contains bulbs and wild flowers, naturalised in the manner recommended by the garden designer William Robinson. Snake's-

The Quarry Garden in about 1900

The view from the tower south over the Croquet Lawn, with Weirwood reservoir and Ashdown Forest in the distance

head fritillaries shoot up in spring, to be followed by orchids in summer. Butterflies, including the Common Blue, are often seen feasting on the flowers.

THE SOUTH LAWN

On the north side, below the Terrace, the lawn is flanked by a border, with old roses trained to trellis-work designed by Webb. The sweet-smelling *Clematis flammula* flowers in the summer.

The north-west edge of the lawn is bounded by a walk to the summer-house (also by Webb) with herbaceous planting separated by clipped box bushes on either side.

Along the south-east side of the lawn are a Tulip Tree (*Liriodendron tulipifera*), the pink form of the Sweet Pepper Bush (*Clethra alnifolia* 'Rosea') and a bank of hardy hybrid rhododendrons.

Near the house there is a triangular bed planted with pink-flowering *Geranium macrorrhizum* with sweetly scented foliage; the curious wooden structure here is a replica of a gong house which the Beales saw on a visit to Japan.

THE BAMBOO GARDEN

Crossing from the South Lawn over the old farm track lined with rhododendrons, which led to the original Standen farm, the visitor arrives at a small Japanese style garden circled with bamboos, including *Sasa palmata* and *Arundinaria murielae*.

THE RHODODENDRON DELL

South-east of the Bamboo Garden are planted groups of rhododendrons including *R. loderi* varieties.

THE ORCHARD

This contains old varieties of apples and pears, as well as mulberries and quince.

THE CROQUET LAWN

Although called the Bowling Green by Webb, this was used by the Beales as a tennis and croquet lawn. Visitors are welcome to play when the hoops have been put out.

Massed rhododendrons cover the slope between the Croquet Lawn summer-house and the south-east corner of the house

To the east is a Dove or Handkerchief Tree (*Davidia involucrata*), with an excellent specimen of Weeping Holly (*Ilex aquifolium* 'Pendula') to the south, and a Monterey Pine (*Pinus radiata*) to the west.

The border north-east of the Green contains a specimen of *Acer palmatum* 'Corallinum' remarkably large for such a slow-growing variety, with shrimp pink leaves in spring. To the front of the border are moisture-loving herbaceous plants such as *Ligularia*, *Houttuynia* and the Mourning Widow (*Geranium phaeum*).

THE ROSE GARDEN

Espalier fruit trees remain from the hedged former kitchen garden, much of which is now used as a car-park. The kitchen garden once had a considerable range of glasshouses that provided fruit and vege-tables for the Beales' London house as well as for Standen. Its undue prominence, once Webb had changed the site for the house, has been to some extent overcome by redesigning its nearest corner as an 'old-fashioned' garden of the type that was favoured in the later nineteenth century. It is planted with rugosa roses, catmint, iris and junipers.

WOODLAND WALKS

HOLLYBUSH WOOD

There is a circular walk of about a mile around the wood, which can be seen from the garden. The wood is a good example of standard oaks under-planted with hazel and sweet chestnut coppice on the site of ancient woodland.

The large depressions at the top of the wood are the result of seventeenth-century farming, when marl, or limey clay, was dug out and spread on the sandy fields as a fertiliser. Iron was smelted in Roman times at the bottom of the wood. Though the site is overgrown, occasionally clinker may be seen in the stream.

WEIRWOOD RESERVOIR

The lane from the lower car-park gives a pleasant walk to Weirwood reservoir. This has a footpath around some of its perimeter fence.

Both these walks can be muddy. The signs with two holly leaves indicate the route round Hollybush Wood.

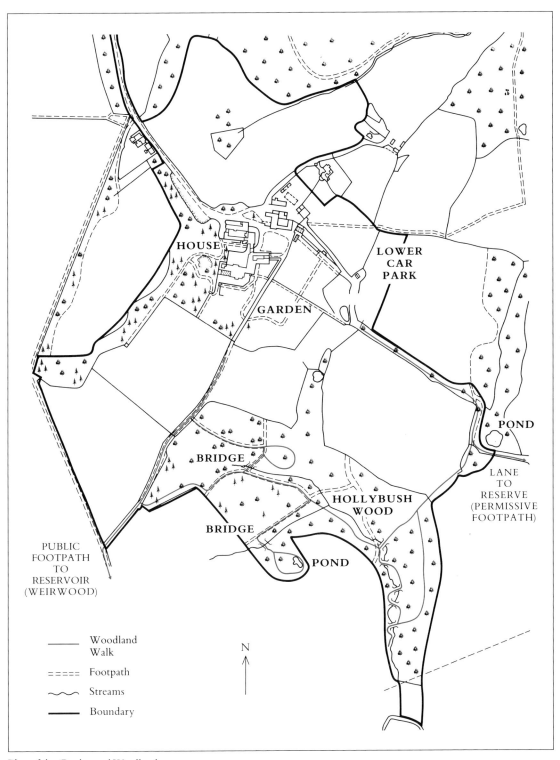

HOUSE

LOWER
CAR
PARK

GARDEN

POND

BRIDGE

HOLLYBUSH
WOOD

LANE
TO
RESERVE
(PERMISSIVE
FOOTPATH)

BRIDGE

POND

PUBLIC
FOOTPATH
TO
RESERVOIR
(WEIRWOOD)

——— Woodland
Walk

===== Footpath

〰〰 Streams

—— Boundary

N
↑

Plan of the Garden and Woodland

BIBLIOGRAPHY

Webb's designs for Standen are in the collections of the RIBA and SPAB. Much other material relating to Standen and the Beale family, including an extensive set of bills for the furnishing of the house, has been deposited in the West Sussex Record Office in Chichester. Joan and Bernard Chibnall's unpublished report on Great Hollybush Farm provides a detailed account of the prehistory of the Standen estate. *Standen Memories*, also unpublished, is a delightful record by James and Margaret's grandchildren of family life at Standen, on which I have drawn heavily for Chapter Five. Dr Sheila Kirk's 1990 PhD thesis on Philip Webb contains the most thorough analysis of Standen.

ASLETT, Clive, *The Last Country Houses*, Yale University Press, 1982.

BARTLETT, John, *English Decorative Ceramics*, Kevin Francis, 1989.

BARTLETT, John, *British Ceramic Art*, Schiffer Publishing, 1993.

BERGESEN, Victoria, *Encyclopaedia of British Art Pottery*, Barrie & Jenkins, 1991.

BRANDON-JONES, John, 'The Work of Philip Webb and Norman Shaw', *Architectural Association Journal*, June 1955, pp.9–21, July 1955, pp.40–5.

BRANDON-JONES, John, 'Philip Webb', in Peter Ferriday ed., *Victorian Architecture*, Cape, 1963, pp.249–65.

BRANDON-JONES, John, 'Arts and Crafts', *Architects Journal Supplement*, December 1984, pp.9–15.

CANNADINE, David, *Lords and Landlords: the Aristocracy and the Towns 1774–1967*, Leicester University Press, 1980, pp.81–225 [for Victorian Edgbaston].

FRANKLIN, Jill, *The Gentleman's Country House and its Plan*, Routledge & Kegan Paul, 1981.

GIROUARD, Mark, 'Standen', *Country Life*, cxlvii, 1970, pp.494–7, 554–7; reprinted in a revised form in *The Victorian Country House*, Yale University Press, 1979, pp.381–9.

GRADIDGE, Roderick, *Dream Houses*, Constable, 1980.

JACK, George, 'An appreciation of Philip Webb', *Architectural Review*, xxxviii, 1915, pp.1–6.

KIRK, Sheila, and CURRY, Rosemary J., *Philip Webb in the North*, Teesside Polytechnic Press, 1984.

KLEIN, Dan, 'Standen: an early paradise', *Connoisseur*, ccviii, December 1981, pp.255–9.

LETHABY, W.R., *Philip Webb and his Work*, Oxford University Press, 1935.

LEVER, Jill, ed., *Catalogue of the Drawings Collection of the Royal Institute of British Architects, T–Z*, Gregg, 1984, pp.184–9 [catalogue of Webb's drawings by T.R. Spence].

OTTEWILL, David, *The Edwardian Garden*, Yale University Press, 1989.

PARRY, Linda, *William Morris Textiles*, Weidenfeld & Nicolson, 1982.

RICARDO, Halsey, 'The House in the Country', *Magazine of Art*, 1900, pp.105–11.

WEAVER, Lawrence, 'Standen', *Country Life*, xxvii, 7 May 1910, pp.666–72.

WEAVER, Lawrence, ed., *The House and its Equipment*, Country Life, 1911.